HIP-HOP SLOP

The Impact of a Dysfunctional Culture

— — —

DeVone Holt

MILTON
MP
PUBLISHING

CHICAGO SPECTRUM PRESS
4824 BROWNSBORO CENTER
LOUISVILLE, KENTUCKY 40207
502-899-1919

Printed in the U.S.A.

To order more copies of this book, contact:

Milton Publishing
PO Box 16745
Louisville, Kentucky 40256
Phone: 502-645-0224
or visit www.hiphopslop.com

10 9 8 7 6 5 4 3 2 1

First Edition

ISBN: 1-58374-080-5

Books are available at quantity discounts when used for educational, business, or sales promotion use.

This book is dedicated to my great-grandfather Milton Dickerson, Sr. who helped ingrain in me a value system that rejects the decadent offerings of contemporary hip-hop.

Thank you for living a life worth modeling.

May your soul rest in peace.

CONTENTS

Acknowledgements

This book would not have materialized without the support of my loving wife, Dionne. Your sacrifices have made me look better than I really am. Thank you, sweetheart, for being my queen.

Thank you, Mother, for always telling me, "You can do it." I did.

To my twelfth-grade English teacher who told me I wouldn't make it, thank you! Your unfounded skepticism produced my activism.

To the St. Stephen Church family, thank you for nurturing me.

To Juan Bell, thanks for making hip-hop fun.

To the greatest theological mind this side of heaven, Dr. Kevin Cosby, thank you for allowing me to witness greatness up close and personal. Your intellectual fingerprints can be found throughout this book.

And last but definitely not least, thank you Jesus Christ. You could have chosen any nappy-headed kid from 39th Street, but you chose me. Thankfully, my life will never be the same.

1

INTRODUCTION

"Hip-hop started out in the heart.
Now everybody's trying to chart."
– Lauryn Hill
"Superstar"

It's a vernacular, garb, music, dance, parties, video

games, art, cars, sports, teeth, liquor, drugs, attitude, tattoos, and

hairdos. It's a lifestyle. It's a culture. It's hip-hop.

Since its inception, the unique traits of hip-hop have

been inextricably linked to the youth in America's urban

communities. Through the culture, young minorities found

something distinctive enough to claim as their own.

Hip-hop is a way of life their parents don't always

understand. It's a movement the government can't regulate. It's

a state of mind teachers often struggle to grasp. And more

importantly, it's a presence that will not go away.

For years, those who didn't understand the culture

made futile attempts to fit it into a tidy box, but hip-hop would

not – and could not – be pigeonholed. It was far too forceful to be contained. Nearly a decade after its birth in the late 1970s, the world began to realize that hip-hop was not simply a music genre, but rather a lifestyle that has the ability to consume a person's every waking hour.

The crossover appeal of the culture helped move it from the heart of America's inner cities to the comfy confines of affluent suburban homes. The buying power of white suburban adolescents, coupled with the passion of their urban counterparts, has nurtured hip-hop to unprecedented levels of prominence.

The influential power of the genre became evident when suburban kids not only purchased rap albums and quoted them lyric for lyric, but when they began to mimic rap artists by wearing their Adidas with no shoelaces, wrapping their heads in colorful bandannas, putting their clothes on backwards, and letting their oversized pants sag off their butts. Their new looks, tastes, and hip-hop attitudes were undeniable proof that the culture had finally "made it."

Hip-hop's successful migration out of the ghetto was a wake-up call for many marketing departments to heed the far-reaching influence of the culture. Consequently, companies that learned to respect the demographic's awesome buying power saturated the retail economy with hip-hop acts, commercials, movies, videos, clothes, books, and attitudes.

What a difference that buying power made. It appears a little R.E.S.P.E.C.T. from Wall Street was all the hip-hop industry needed to solidify itself as more than a passing fad. Now, an industry that was built on the strength of America's youth and had the wherewithal to tightly weave its way into the fabric of the nation's economy is a powerful, multifaceted force that cannot be overlooked.

In the year 2001, hip-hop accounted for more than $1.5 billion of the music industry's record sales, clearly making it one of the world's most influential genres. Hip-hop clothing lines Sean John, Phat Farm, FUBU, Karl Kani, and Rocawear complemented those numbers by earning more than $800 million. Still to boot were the $600 million collective earnings of hip-hop magazines *Vibe*, *The Source*, and *XXL*. The combined sum of these figures is still only a fraction of the wealth hip-hop was able to generate over the course of one year. These statistics don't include the many millions of dollars collected via hip-hop movies and concerts.

What's more startling is the fact that these numbers stand alone with no smoke-and-mirror gimmicks. They scream success! Victory! Importance! Longevity! Youth! And, most importantly, power! They tell one of America's greatest rags-to-riches stories. Next to the NFL and the NBA, hip-hop has produced more young black millionaires than any other legitimate industry in the world.

This culture that once served as rock-and-roll's disavowed understudy is now acting as mentor to the icons of yesteryear. It might be well argued that Michael Jackson's staying power over the last decade can be partially attributed to his ability to successfully flirt with hip-hop. On his last three albums the King of Pop collaborated with some of the most well-known hip-hop artists and producers.

Like Jackson, other seasoned veterans have also found in hip-hop a life preserver for careers drowning in the sea of oblivion. The Queen of Soul, Aretha Franklin, owes a great deal of credit to Lauryn Hill for reintroducing her to the Billboard charts with the song "A Rose is Still a Rose." As hip-hop's bestselling female artist, Hill expanded her territory into traditional R&B by writing, producing, singing background, and directing the video for the hit song.

Include those names with others like Justin Timberlake, Britney Spears, N*SYNC, Backstreet Boys, Jennifer Lopez, Madonna, Jesse Jackson, Ben Stiller, Yolanda Adams, Kirk Franklin, Anthrax, and Aerosmith, and it becomes apparent that hip-hop is no respecter of boundaries.

Hip-hop has evolved from the blighted corners of New York City to luxurious executive towers in Los Angeles and has blossomed into one of the nation's most influential industries. Once treated as a stepchild, hip-hop now commands attention. When it speaks, people listen.

This book will take a microscopic look at what hip-hop says when it does speak and dissect the impact it has on its listeners and society at large. It will examine how hip-hop has simultaneously broken down barriers and built up blockades in the areas of racism, sexism, materialism, anti-intellectualism, violence, and social responsibilities.

This book will explore the route hip-hop took to move from a harmless novelty act to a threatening, ubiquitous culture. It will analyze the excuses that have prevented hip-hop from fulfilling its greatest potential. And it will detail the rationale of hip-hop fans who swear by the music as well as reveal the frustration of those who know the culture is dancing on a dangerous, slippery slope.

While it's important to understand what this book is intended to do, it is just as significant to understand what it is not designed to do. *Hip-Hop Slop* is not intended to run hip-hop out of business or end the careers of controversial hip-hop pundits. It might be thought that this book is intended to censor every belligerent rap artist who makes a hit record. Some might even think that *Hip-Hop Slop* has found a nemesis in pop culture. These assessments couldn't be more inaccurate.

The truth is, hip-hop has been a great friend to me over the years. It shouted with me as CA$H MONEY and Marvelous told all the "ugly people to be quiet." It cried with me through the lyrics of Tupac Shakur's "Shed So Many Tears" when my cousin Nick was murdered. It put money in my pocket by making hit records for me to spin at parties. And through the rhythmic teachings of KRS-ONE, it helped me retain the Bible better than any of my adolescent Sunday school classes.

But lately I can't help but notice that the friend that nurtured me as a young fan now needs to be nurtured through a damaging image and reputation crisis of its own. Through the next eight chapters, this book will take a thorough look at the culture (much like a parent would a dysfunctional child) and offer loving recommendations to confront, correct, and ultimately redirect one of America's most creative movements.

(WARNING: Because *Hip-Hop Slop* critiques the graphic nature of hip-hop culture, an *"Explicit Content"* warning is necessary for this book.)

1

HIP-HOP HOLOCAUST

"If you can write a nation's stories,
you need not worry about who writes the laws."
– Adolf Hitler

Those who are intimately familiar with rap music know that its lyrical content has taken on a new attitude since the 1980's. In a twenty-year span, the genre has moved from the mostly harmless lyrics of groups like Run-D.M.C, Slick Rick, Doug E. Fresh, and Heavy D to today's rarely redemptive lyrics of sex, drugs, violence, and hedonistic pleasures from acts like Snoop Dogg, Dr. Dre, Ludacris, and D12. The moral bridge that separates the current era from the 80's is a vast one that took years to build and is worth exploring.

As it is with any radical departure from a cultural standard, an evolution must occur. Such is the case with hip-hop. We didn't merely wake up one day to suddenly learn that hip-hop music had plummeted in the way of ethics, values, and integrity. The culture underwent a five-step evolutionary process that charted the course for the deviant standard prevalent in contemporary hip-hop.

The first trend in hip-hop's evolution was shock. In the mid-1980's, artists such as the 2 Live Crew, Too Short, N.W.A., Ice-T, and the Geto Boys emerged on the scene with their explicit and lewd tales of sex, drugs, murder and mayhem. As these artists took big, bold steps to move beyond the unwritten rules of cultural acceptance, parents, politicians, and even some rap fans couldn't believe what they were hearing. To many, these new renegade hip-hop artists had broken a sacred code of decency. What ensued were highly publicized petitions to ban this new onslaught of in-your-face hip-hop.

However, with limited victories and a saturated market of "gangsta rappers," America moved relatively swiftly into the second phase of hip-hop deviancy: numbness. Hip-hop fans and haters alike were soon inundated by lewd artists with explicit messages looking to cash in on the new lucrative age of moral bankruptcy and limited creativity.

The barrage of substandard hip-hop acts began to beat at America's values until the industry had numbed the nation's senses like that of a boxer who has taken too many jabs to the nose. Soon, the anesthetized minds of hip-hop's young fans began to question what they should believe and believe what they should question. What once was right for many of them soon became wrong, and what was wrong became right.

This new counterculture would soon spawn the third stage of hip-hop deviancy: ridiculous comparisons. As rap acts like Snoop Dogg, Dr. Dre, Tupac Shakur, and the Notorious B.I.G. began to grow increasingly popular, a common argument of those seeking to protect their image and investment was that many other forms of entertainment were worse than rap music.

Nelson George, a long-time hip-hop aficionado, championed this theory with his attempt to legitimize the lyrics of Tupac and the Notorious B.I.G. by comparing them to the cinematic work of director Martin Scorsese. He argues that Scorsese's gangster movies are celebrated "violent masterworks" yet "Tupac and Biggie were labeled gangsta rappers in their obituaries."

This type of bait-and-switch has been integral in convincing people that today's music isn't so bad. This philosophy of passing the buck attempts to shift the blame for the behavior of unscrupulous rappers to someone or something else to avoid deserved criticism.

It's similar to the rationale of the speeding driver who complains to police that there are murderers on the loose, yet he's being hassled for simply driving over the speed limit. While speeding isn't usually a serious offense, it is a punishable crime that is responsible for thousands of deaths per year. Ignoring speeding, as a result, is a more dishonorable act than actually speeding.

Tolerance is the fourth stage of hip-hop deviancy. The "oh well, that's just the way it is" attitude has permeated the mindset of many Americans and ruined their resolve to challenge the status quo. In efforts to promote tolerance among critics, hip-hop pundits often declare, "If you don't like it, don't buy," or "No one is makes you listen to it." These empty rationalizations too often have been successful in increasing America's tolerance levels for gangster rap, which ultimately makes it easier for the genre to maintain its stronghold on society.

The fifth and final stage of hip-hop deviancy is hostility. In this stage, an amazing reversal occurs that creates a constituency that grows increasingly intolerant of people who don't share their open-mindedness. Hip-hop pundits use any opportunity they can to discredit and wound anyone who doesn't share their thoughts and views at this juncture.

One of the more prominent examples of this reverse hostility was displayed by one of hip-hop's most glorified icons in an attempt to discredit an aggressive gangster rap critic. Tupac, creator of the "Thug Life" image, vehemently displayed his disdain for activist C. Delores Tucker in his song "How Do You Want It" when he rapped, "Delores Tucker you's a motherfucker. Instead of trying to help a nigga you destroy a brother. Worse than the others."

These stages of shock, numbness, ridiculous comparisons, tolerance, and hostility have led the culture into an unprecedented state of ethical treason. In this state, morals and responsibilities are quickly becoming things of the past as new levels of immorality take residence in hip-hop's world of grit and grim.

And while the world is more than a half-century removed from the dreadful Jewish Holocaust that was responsible for inexcusably murdering millions of Jews, its trends of corruption are laced throughout the history of gangster rap. Unbeknownst to many enthusiasts, Germany's patterns of destruction have insidiously resurfaced in the hip-hop industry.

The Birth of a Movement

The Jewish Holocaust can be traced to one man, Adolf Hitler, whose initial intent as a young advocate was to improve the social and financial conditions of his depressed country. Unfortunately for millions of people, what started as an admirable cause eventually became known as the world's greatest atrocity.

Though rap music doesn't have a dictator, its gangster genre can be traced to radical social-conscious rappers who wanted nothing more than to have a voice in the plight to improve social conditions in their deprived communities. Artists like Grandmaster Flash and the Furious Five, KRS-ONE, Public Enemy, X-Clan, Run- D.M.C, and Queen Latifah played

13

integral roles in laying the groundwork for the onset of commercial gangster rap.

Though these artists typically promote peace and equality, if their aggressive lyrics aren't carefully deciphered they might sometimes be mistaken for irresponsible, riotous messages. Ambiguous song titles, including "Criminal Minded," "Fight The Power," "Heed the Word of the Brother," and "Raising Hell," indeed send mixed messages. Similarly, lyrics like "It's like a jungle sometimes; it makes me wonder how I keep from going under" and "Who you calling a bitch!" can be misinterpreted.

The gangster era was born when artists looking to build on this aggressive social-conscious style began to stretch its boundaries by eliminating the redemptive qualities once inherent in the lyrics. Tupac is the quintessential example of this transformation. As a budding star, his first album was replete with aggressive songs and messages of empowerment, social justice, and graphic tales of ghetto struggles that incited advocacy.

However, in his later albums he crossed the thin line that separates revolutionaries from gangsters as he nearly abandoned his stance for social justice to give birth to the Thug Life image. Other would-be rap revolutionaries found themselves dancing on the same thin line and eventually siding with an army of thugs who collectively threaten the decency of a nation by continuing to "push the envelope."

Honing the Message

As a young advocate, Hitler crossed the line of simple advocacy to passionate anti-Semitism by subscribing to dangerously radical social philosophies (most notably Nazism) that initially brewed in relative obscurity with little fanfare. He honed his gift to passionately articulate his new fascistic ideologies as a low-ranking political speaker in the military, where he practiced delivering speeches to the returning prisoners of war. It was only when he was given a national platform and immense power that his sordid philosophies gained legions of misguided followers.

In a similar vein, a small fraction of young rappers subscribed to the art of studio gangsterism in the music's adolescent years. With limited commercialization, gangster rappers like Ice-T, the Geto Boys, and Eazy-E initiated their careers and honed their messages by marketing their venomous lyrics to a relatively small nucleus of fans. Comparable to the formative years of the Nazi regime, gangster rap was built on the passion of a small number of supporters who were waved off as harmless threats to society by majority groups.

However, when gangster rap pundits like Dr. Dre, Sean "P. Diddy" Combs, Russell Simmons, and Tony Draper began to land executive-level jobs at prominent record companies or launch successful record labels, they used their national platforms to enticingly espouse their messages of violence, irresponsible sex, drugs, alcohol, pimping, and other lewd behaviors. Their national (and often international) stage allowed them to cast a much larger net, spawning today's gangster rap phenomenon.

Like Hitler and his Nazi philosophy, gangster rap didn't become overwhelmingly dangerous until it assumed a broad-reaching platform. And unfortunately for many, at that stage the irreparable damage had been done.

Follow Me

Immediately upon seizing his national stage, Hitler used his influence to persuade his new converts to forsake their moral compasses to adopt his ideology of hatred and persecution. He understood that his vision of world dominance would never be fulfilled if he could not convince millions of Germans to jettison their ethical standards and focus their efforts on shamelessly eradicating Jews.

The gangster rap genre thrives on its ability to build a fan base that, like the Nazi-era Germans, willingly adopts its counterculture philosophies. Many of its fans were reared in households that subscribed to traditional wholesome values of respect, honesty, love, integrity, and the Golden Rule. The risk of compromising those values, however, significantly increases as fans candidly flirt with the music. The savvy marketing ploys and catchy phrases in the lyrics can subliminally spur subtle renouncements of traditional values.

This is especially true when consideration is given to the sophisticated campaigns employed by record companies to anoint their lyrics as sacred doctrine. They often rival and surpass the aggressive tactics used in modern American presidential elections, which makes it increasingly difficult for unstable gangster rap fans to adhere to a core set of traditional values.

Thug Passion

Hitler's ability to combine an effective, rehearsed speaking style with apparent sincerity and undeniable resolve appealed to a wide variety of people.

Likewise, gangster rappers have found large audiences for their messages of misogyny, drug use, violence, police hatred, and dangerous hedonistic pleasures via their passionate displays. Few fans would argue against the claim that Tupac was hip-hop's most passionate rapper. His apparent sincerity in songs like "Keep Your Head Up" (an ode to troubled black women) and passionate tirades in songs like "Hit 'Em Up" (a venomous message of hatred and graphic violence towards his professed enemies) serve as magnets for fans attracted to his zealous commitment to those themes.

Tupac's sincerity — whether right or wrong — was one of his greatest assets in an industry that invests in the authenticity of its artists. If you're a gangster rapper and say you're from the streets, you better be from the streets. If you say you know what it's like in jail, you better have spent some time there. Vanilla Ice suffered a short-lived rap career after it was learned that he didn't live the life he professed.

This type of fan-driven demand for sincerity has challenged gangster rappers to ensure their reality penetrates their lyrics and their records match their reality. What has transpired is an enormous fan base for gangster rappers like 50 Cent with lengthy police files and dysfunctional lives.

Can I Get an Amen?

Though many supported Hitler and the Nazi regime, not as many subscribed wholeheartedly to all of the party's fascist ideologies. It was with great cunning that Hitler was able to attract millions to his cause by catering to their many isolated concerns with emotional appeals absent of any intellectual reasoning. In his elaborate messages of world dominance through hatred, war, and deceit, many found enough attention given to their personal interests that they bought into the Nazi philosophy.

N.W.A. (Niggas With Attitudes) got the attention of millions of African-Americans with their song "Fuck Tha

Police." The song explicitly captured the frustrations of the many victims of police brutality and racial profiling, who until that time heard no artists address their concerns with such fervor.

Finding a group to speak on their behalf with a national platform encouraged many to unconditionally support N.W.A. even though they eventually would be recognized as "the world's most dangerous group." Although their songs like "Dope Man," "Gangsta Gangsta," "If It Ain't Ruff," and "Parental Discretion Iz Advised" didn't resonate with social-conscience fans, their no-holds-barred social commentaries in "Express Yourself" and the aforementioned "Fuck Tha Police" helped legitimize them as an important group to people who would have otherwise written them off.

Money Talks

Hitler's revolutionary message of German empowerment came at a time when the nation was undergoing significant financial troubles. His words of encouragement gave hope to many who were looking for a way out a depression.

When gangster rap exploded on the scene in the late 1980s and early 1990s, there was a lull in the music industry. This new genre, however, generated new dollars and was thus embraced by those who were fighting financial depression in the

19

music industry. Hip-hop was a life preserver for the industry, just as many expected Nazism to be for Germany.

The Children Are the Future

Once Hitler and the Nazi party were in power they began to institute practices that influenced youth to spend their free time involved with the party. The goal was to traditionalize Nazism by indoctrinating people into the party at young ages.

That same philosophy is prevalent in hip-hop. The thirty-year-old and under fan base purchases the music, watches the videos, attends the concerts, and mimics the artists in greater proportions than any other demographic.

Without the commitment of America's youth, hip-hop would dissipate into obscurity. The purchasing power of the ten- to twenty-nine-year-old demographic is far too great for the industry to ignore. According to the Recording Industry Association of America's consumer profile, the twenty-nine-year-old and under demographic purchases nearly 50 percent of all the music sold in the nation.

And more importantly, for posterity's sake, the youth of America are more critical than ever in keeping the spirit of hip-hop alive. That in part explains why record labels are investing significant resources to develop young rap artists like Bow Wow, Lil' Romeo, Lil' Zane, Lil' J, and Lil' Wayne.

The Shutout

When Hitler assumed control of Germany's influential institutions he ensured that people who didn't embrace his philosophies wouldn't benefit from the life-improving services they offered. Jews could not get loans from banks to buy homes or enroll in educational institutions. His intent was to weed out all those who were outside of his liking and only support those who enhanced his vision.

Hip-hop record label executives like Simmons (Def Jam), Combs (Bad Boy Entertainment), Dr. Dre (Aftermath), Jermaine Dupri (So So Def), Suge Knight (Death Row), Jay-Z (Roc-A-Fella), and Master P (No Limit) all appear to have adopted some semblance of Hitler's philosophy of exclusion. As overseers of these influential record labels, they only sign and market artists who share their rough-edged taste in music. An artist with a polished look and an encouraging message likely will be exiled from these institutions of music like the Jews were once cast away from Germany's banks and schools.

Allied Forces

Hitler knew it was impossible for Germany to fulfill his vision of world dominance without the support of other countries. Therefore, he facilitated Germany's alliances with

Italy, Japan, and the Soviet Union to accomplish his goal. Similarly, the partnerships in gangster rap have helped reinforce its stronghold on the entertainment industry and expand the boundaries of the music genre by transcending into movies, television, Web sites, fashion, and pornography.

The Intimidation Factor

Lastly, once Germany became a major power, Hitler used the country's great resources to intimidate other countries. Nearly seventy years later, those same intimidation tactics have unsurprisingly permeated the hip-hop industry.

The history of the gangster rap movement is laced with violent tales. For example, it is highly rumored that Knight, a six feet three inches tall, 300+-pound former college football player, dangled Vanilla Ice by his feet from the balcony of a multistory hotel room until he agreed to release the publishing rights to his hit song "Ice Ice Baby." It has also been said that Knight threatened now deceased rapper and record company owner Eazy-E into relinquishing his rights to Dr. Dre so that the super producer might partner with Knight to create Death Row Records.

Combs made headline news for his vicious attack on industry executive Steve Stout for not agreeing to delete his unfavorable appearance from a music video. And in 2004, famed rapper Jay-Z will end his probation sentence for stabbing entertainment executive Lance "Un" Rivera at a nightclub.

———————

While the aforementioned parallels of the Jewish Holocaust and hip-hop don't imply that the powers that be in the entertainment industry have the same intent as Hitler and the Nazi regime, they should serve as a forewarning. If it transpires, the main objective of the Hip-Hop Holocaust will not be to eliminate races but to rid people of their moral priorities by discrediting messages of responsible entertainment and promoting the reckless practices common in gangster rap.

That means this war on moral principles will not be won on bloodstained battlefields like World War II. Instead, it will be won in the hearts of men, women, and children who commit to fighting for their beliefs.

For hip-hop pundits unfamiliar with this history lesson, it is important to know that Hitler and the Nazi regime eventually succumbed to the pressure of an alliance of armies committed to protecting the freedoms and values that Germany threatened.

Currently in America, many citizens, organizations, churches, and even government entities are pondering how to defuse the entertainment industry's threatening practices. As these entities begin to understand the ultimate power that rests in forming alliances, their ability to lend credence to the phrase "those who don't know their history are destined to repeat it" gains greater significance than ever.

2

BABYSITTER FOR HIRE

*"I came to save a new generation of babies from
parents who don't raise them cause they're lazy."*
– Eminem
"Fight Music"

Since its inception, hip-hop has been a youth
movement. Over the course of three decades, the genre has
thrived on the passionate interest of teenagers and young adults
who purchase, defend, and emulate nearly everything produced
in its name.

While there are older fans who support the culture, ten-
to twenty-four-year-olds give hip-hop life. In it, they've found a
religion that gives them principles to live by. As a result, they
purchase the albums, wear the clothes, and embrace the
attitudes in greater proportions than any other demographic. For
many of them, hip-hop is their only way of life. It's an identity
for them to claim until they find their own. And the industry
professionals who recognize this demographic as a cash cow

have successfully marketed their goods to America's youths, who in turn have made an unprecedented commitment to consume them.

A 1999 study by the Kaiser Family Foundation revealed some startling statistics about the media intake of children ages two through eighteen. The study, *Kids & Media @ The New Millennium,* discovered that a "typical American child spends an average of more than thirty-eight hours a week--nearly five and a half hours a day (5:29)--consuming media outside of school. That amount is even higher--nearly six and three-quarter hours a day (6:43)--for kids eight and older." On average, according to the survey, American children spend nearly the equivalent of a full-time workweek under the influence of some television show, Web site, video game, movie, music video, singer/rapper, celebrity, or writer not positioned to determine their best interests.

The sad tale in these statistics is that the average American child is influenced more by the media than anything else. Many children spend more of their waking moments under the influence of media than with their parents. Even fewer spend more time with a mentor. And they certainly spend less than thirty-eight hours a week in class or church.

Couple those statistics with the fact that teenagers and young adults have made hip-hop one of the leading music genres, and it becomes apparent that the youths of our nation (particularly urban youths) spend an enormous amount of time under the influence of hip-hop. The messages laced in the lyrics, the demeanors portrayed in the videos, and the attitudes in the performers' interviews are infiltrating impressionable minds like nothing else.

There's no doubt about it. Hip-hop is babysitting our future leaders. This observation begs the question, "Is this culture qualified to look after our children?"

Ask parents this question, and you are certain to get several responses similar to the one a pastor received when he asked a heathen if he could identify the two most prevalent problems Americans face. Snidely, the heathen responded, "I don't know, and I don't care."

Little did he know his flippant reply was the precise answer to the pastor's question. For decades, ignorance and apathy have been the greatest impediments to solving our nation's social ills. Consider the clear sign of ignorance and the devastating ramifications that rest in the fact that many parents don't know what their children are reading, watching, or hearing. Or consider the undeniable sign of apathy that rears its ugly head when some parents learn that their children are consuming unhealthy hip-hop yet remain indifferent.

Not knowing and not caring about the effect hip-hop has on our children makes it impossible for some to accurately critique the culture. Additionally, these faults speak volumes about our society's lack of instinctive interest to protect our youths from harmful influences.

27

During my routine jog one day, I watched a bird viciously attack a squirrel for poking its head into a nest of eggs. With little knowledge of the squirrel's intent or true desire of its heart, the bird saw the intrusion as a threat to its offspring and risked its life to give the hatchlings a healthy chance to mature. We as humans, however, sometimes appear to have lost our animal instinct to protect our youths from such intrusions. We mistakenly rely on the government to protect the mental and social health of our children by tightly monitoring the content disseminated for their consumption. Yet, the sad reality is that over the past four decades the government has grown increasingly lax in its efforts to monitor media content.

Nearly fifty years ago it was uncommon to see a married couple sleep in the same bed on television or hear profanity on the radio. On *I Love Lucy* in the 1950s, Ricky and Lucy very rarely displayed any passionate emotions for each other – let alone considered sleeping in the same bed. And just twenty years ago a curse word uttered on the radio would have raised the eyebrows of the most sophisticated street hustlers.

Today, a pendulum swing in media tolerance has softened the market. It's commonplace to witness unclothed adulterous couples locking lips and bumping hips during prime-time hours on network television. Likewise, it's typical to hear the words "ass," "damn," "bitch," and "nigger" broadcast across many of the nation's urban radio stations.

Sufficed to say, the many parents who hold the government responsible for filtering media ultimately render their children more vulnerable to harmful intrusions than the common bird. On some levels their lack of instinctive reaction to personally protect their children says that they are less than animals and tells a revealing story about the health of our nation.

———————

When Robert Tools, the world's first recipient of a self-contained artificial heart, was in the early stages of recuperation, the doctors carefully measured his health by monitoring his appetite. That's because the presence of an appetite suggests that a weak person's body is interested in strengthening itself. Conversely, the lack of an appetite is a clear sign of an unhealthy person because the body no longer desires its source of strength.

People suffering from heartbreak, bereavement, depression, shock, or gross preoccupation are highly susceptible to loss of appetite. It is the latter group who severely jeopardize the health of the nation's youth. Their obsession with trivial concerns ruins their appetite to ward off the negative content that inundates the next generation of leaders and thus legitimizes our status as a "sick society." Furthermore, their lack of an appetite to fight for healthier mediums has weakened society's defense mechanism and opened the floodgates to a host of salacious material and acts.

This questionable material is now quantifiable, thanks to an innovative service that dissects the lyrical content of popular songs. *LyricScan* tracks uses of profanity and references to sex, drugs, alcohol, violence, and contemptuous behavior in the music that influences legions of impressionable listeners. A *LyricScan* filter of the 2001 Source Awards Single of the Year nominees produced the following results:

Single of the Year 2001 Source Awards LyricScan Search							
Artist/ Song	Sexual References	Uses of Profanity	Drug References	Alcohol References	Racial Epithets	Violent References	Contemptuous References
Eminem feat. Dido "Stan"	Educational: 0 Subtle: 1 Lewd: 0	24	Condoned: 0 Denounced: 0 Indifferent: 1	Responsible: 0 Irresponsible: 0 Indifferent: 2	0	Condoned: 0 Denounced: 1 Indifferent: 12	Condoned: 0 Denounced: 0 Indifferent: 6
Ja Rule feat. Lil'Mo & Vita "Put It On Me"	Educational: 0 Subtle: 15 Lewd: 0	1	Condoned: 0 Denounced: 0 Indifferent: 0	Responsible: 0 Irresponsible: 0 Indifferent: 0	0	Condoned: 0 Denounced: 0 Indifferent: 0	Condoned: 5 Denounced: 0 Indifferent: 0
Outkast "Ms. Jackson"	Educational: 1 Subtle: 1 Lewd: 1	5	Condoned: 0 Denounced: 0 Indifferent: 0	Responsible: 0 Irresponsible: 0 Indifferent: 0	0	Condoned: 0 Denounced: 0 Indifferent: 2	Condoned: 0 Denounced: 0 Indifferent: 0
Nelly "Country Grammar"	Educational: 0 Subtle: 1 Lewd: 1	10	Condoned: 13 Denounced: 0 Indifferent: 0	Responsible: 0 Irresponsible: 4 Indifferent: 0	24	Condoned: 3 Denounced: 0 Indifferent: 0	Condoned: 12 Denounced: 0 Indifferent: 0
Ludacris "Southern Hospitality"	Educational: 0 Subtle: 3 Lewd: 16	19	Condoned: 3 Denounced: 0 Indifferent: 0	Responsible: 0 Irresponsible: 1 Indifferent: 0	18	Condoned: 2 Denounced: 0 Indifferent: 0	Condoned: 16 Denounced: 0 Indifferent: 0
Mystikal "Shake Ya Ass"	Educational: 0 Subtle: 21 Lewd: 12	52	Condoned: 1 Denounced: 0 Indifferent: 0	Responsible: 0 Irresponsible: 0 Indifferent: 1	11	Condoned: 1 Denounced: 0 Indifferent: 0	Condoned: 9 Denounced: 0 Indifferent: 0
Total	Educational: 1 Subtle: 42 Lewd: 30	111	Condoned: 17 Denounced: 0 Indifferent: 1	Responsible: 0 Irresponsible: 5 Indifferent: 3	53	Condoned: 6 Denounced: 1 Indifferent: 14	Condoned: 42 Denounced: 0 Indifferent: 6

The statistics in this *LyricScan* study (accessible at www.AAOReport.com) represent the industry's best-selling commercial products, which ironically now hover at the lowest level of decency in the genre's history. The consistent decline in these statistics over the years is hard evidence of America's waning appetite to protect its young hip-hop diehards.

As startling as these findings are, they don't represent the worst of the culture. There is a vast market of less popular rap groups and R&B hip-hop artists with cult followings that espouse even more venomous messages.

For instance, the rap group UGK (Underground Kingz) has sold more than 1 million records with lyrics similar to those in the duo's song "Murder":

> *Now take a look at the bigger nigga,*
> *Malt liquor swigger, player hater, ditch digger,*
> *Figure my hair trigger*
> *Give a hot one to your liver, you shiver shake and quiver,*
> *I'm frivolous if a nigga get wetter than a river,*
> *For what it's worth, it's the birth of some niggas doin' dirt,*
> *Fuck the first thing in a skirt and make the pussy hurt,*
> *It's that Master, hit the Swisher faster than you fever-blister*
> *bastards.*

Many of the most successful commercial hip-hop songs of the late 1980s and early 1990s — songs like "It Takes Two" (Rob Base and D.J. E-Z Rock), "Whoomp! There It Is" (Tag Team), "U Can't Touch This" (MC Hammer), "Parents Just Don't

Understand" (Jazzy Jeff and the Fresh Prince), and "Jump" (Kris Kross) — collectively don't contain as many racial epithets, uses of profanity, or references to sex and contemptuous behavior as 2001 Source Single of the Year nominee "Shake Ya Ass" by Mystikal.

The dramatic decline in rap's lyrical content over the past ten years is an obvious indication that America's tolerance has steadily increased as its level of apathy has soared. It appears that America has turned its back on hip-hop's most ardent fans and relinquished its responsibility to "protect and serve" those incapable of protecting themselves.

As it stands today, our children have been placed in the inadequate care of hip-hop. In many instances, it has filled the role as guardian, spiritual advisor, mentor, and teacher to its immature listeners. But too often in those capacities hip-hop has neglected their social, spiritual, intellectual, and health needs.

———

Socially, hip-hop hasn't prepared its young understudies for life after baggy/sagging pants, bandannas, broken English, gold-grill teeth, and cornrows. The freedoms that come with the boundless energies of hip-hop are only tolerated by society as passing youthful fads that are expected to become memories of rebellious adolescent years. However, when a person's embrace of hip-hop is carried over into adulthood, that person is likely to face difficulty fitting into society at large because they've lost the youthful naivety often attributed to the juvenile culture. Typically, adults who refuse to loosen their tight grip on hip-hop can anticipate difficulty landing decent-paying, mid-level jobs. They might also plan for a low level of acceptance among peers who have matured beyond the frivolous concerns often associated with hip-hop.

A common misunderstanding among young hip-hop fans is that they can be embraced like the wealthy rap stars who wear hip-hop clothes everywhere, speak Ebonics all the time, and maintain contemptuous attitudes. They don't realize that these rap artists are anomalies who are tolerated because they have occupations conducive to such behavior and often times have reached an elite level of fame and wealth.

But juxtaposed to reality, hip-hop gives the false perception that anyone can abandon the unwritten rules of society that sometimes unfairly dictate who will and won't succeed. But that won't fly in the real world. The gangster rapper B.G. told his listeners in the song "Ride or Die" to "play the game how it goes." Unfortunately he and many other rappers haven't taught their listeners to play life's game of advanced survival. Rather, they've taught them to fumble along at life's novice level by promoting violence, degrading women and themselves, risking their freedom by glamorizing the grimy world of drug use and drug sales, equating self-worth with net worth, and downgrading sex to a mere caveman-like experience.

Spiritually, hip-hop has a tendency to leave its followers malnourished. With the exception of the Lauryn Hills, the Goodie Mobs, and the growing number of Christian rappers, modern hip-hop icons typically lead their followers on a wild-goose chase for happiness void of any heavenly ordained guidance.

Too often hip-hop fans have bowed before the god of materialism only to learn that a house isn't a home, expensive vacations can't guarantee rest, luxury transportation doesn't constitute smooth sailing, and bling-bling jewelry won't necessarily brighten their futures. They have worshiped the uncertain god of money only to find that it can't buy love and true friendship, can't ensure peace, and can't promise loyalty. And they have submitted to the god of promiscuity only to enter the uncomfortable worlds of venereal disease, heartbreak, abortions, unplanned children, and unnecessary death.

Contrary to the doctrine of contemporary hip-hop, former rap megastar Ma$e — now Christian pastor Rev. Mason Betha — said it wasn't until he relinquished all of his hip-hop status symbols that he found true peace and happiness. His departure from the popular culture at the height of his career caught the attention of nearly everyone associated with hip-hop but has remained an anomaly.

———————

Intellectually, hip-hop has stunted the mental capacities of its listeners by dwelling in a pit of non-stimulating subject matter. Adults often rightfully warn children that smoking cigarettes can stunt their physical growth. Unfortunately, not as many adults warn children that a constant intake of frivolous entertainment can stunt their mental growth. A fixation on a genre built around braggadocios lyrics, sexual promiscuity, gangster mentalities, hedonistic passions, and drug and alcohol abuse does little to promote intellectual aptitude.

While it is inappropriate to solely blame hip-hop for the plunge in today's intellectual aptitudes, the culture can't be removed from the equation that helped produce the result. Overlooking the distracting influences hip-hop has on its listeners is like ignoring the role money plays in high school athletes' decisions to forgo college and turn pro. In many cases, the lure of multimillion dollar contracts is powerful enough to cause high-school students to skip the maturation process of college and seek the instant gratification of professional sports. Similarly, the lack of intellectual stimuli in today's hip-hop culture causes its followers to not prioritize their intellectual pursuits but rather master in mediocrity.

It is often asked, particularly in the African-American community, if today's generation could ever produce another social, spiritual, and intellectual leader like Martin Luther King, Jr. Statically, the chances of that happening grow increasingly slimmer with today's proliferating constituency of hip-hop fans bent on maintaining the culture's status quo.

From a health perspective, hip-hop has done relatively little to encourage its listeners to protect themselves from AIDS, untimely death, violence, drugs, and alcohol. The *LyricScan* study revealed that all of the six songs nominated for the 2001 Source Single of the Year award promoted and glorified at least one irresponsible, health-threatening act. As mentioned before, these top-six songs merely represent a small fraction of songs and acts with similar themes. Collectively, they have contributed to the creation of America's most murderous demographic (twelve- to twenty-four-year-olds), fastest-growing AIDS population (young adult African-Americans), and youngest drug and alcohol abusers.

"What They See Is What They'll Be"
– 100 Black Men

A glimpse at hip-hop for someone completely unfamiliar with the culture would likely result in the belief that the youths of America are only concerned with sex, drugs, violence, money, and selfish gain. That's because these are the images that inundate media outlets where the average American youth spends nearly forty hours a week. These images and themes have significantly influenced the attitudes and behaviors of the hip-hop generation. Therefore, today's youths are forced to confront subject matter typically reserved for adults because no hard line exists in hip-hop to differentiate adult content from adolescent content.

Daily, America's influential minds are subjected to crass, complex, and mature adult material. Consequently, they prematurely abandon the innocence of their adolescence for the often-scandalous escapades of the adult world. Their time in hip-hop has improperly exposed them to dangerous material and situations that interrupts their natural maturation process. To help them reclaim their innocence, America's adults must learn to embrace their animal instinct to protect our vulnerable offspring from the preying babysitter called hip-hop.

3

IT AIN'T MY FAULT
(Did I Do That?)

"I think young people can make choices
of what they can listen to."
−   Russell Simmons

Damon Dash, CEO of Roc-A-Fella Records, made a statement uncharacteristic of most hip-hop profiteers: "Roc-A-Fella fucked up hip-hop."

Although Roc-A-Fella — home to one of rap's most acclaimed performers, Jay-Z — can't be solely credited for damaging hip-hop, Dash's confession is an anomaly among hip-hop insiders who usually defend their participation in the genre at any cost.

Employing passionate defense tactics is typical protocol for hip-hop zealots seeking to protect the questionable themes prevalent in the culture. In many cases, their claims are baseless but seem to satisfy those who pledge their undying support.

That's due, in part, to the fact that the legitimacy of their comments and arguments are rarely thoroughly explored.

A glaring example of such an oversight is the intent of the highly publicized 2001 Hip-Hop Summit commissioned by hip-hop mogul Russell Simmons. As one of the most influential figures in hip-hop, Simmons lured approximately 300 top artists, executives, politicians, and community leaders to discuss the state of the industry and suggest steps to improve it.

Among the topics discussed and agreed upon during the summit were the needs for greater political involvement and activism, a mentoring program for new artists, hip-hop think tanks, and guidelines to establish consistent use of "Explicit Lyrics" warning labels.

Unfortunately, an oft-repeated comment by Simmons about the event reveals that the efforts of those at the summit were on the right tracks but definitely aboard the wrong train.

"I want to say this because a lot of people have been asking am I intending to clean up rap. I absolutely am not looking to clean up anything," Simmons audaciously admitted.

With that statement, he posed an interesting dichotomy for those who sought to understand the purpose of a summit that was entitled "Taking Back Responsibility." If its sponsor chose not to use the venue to "clean up" a wounded industry that can't be healed without responsible purification of its lyrics, images, and behavior, why meet?

These ambiguous facts beg an answer to the question: What was Simmons' true intent for the summit? Maybe we'll never know. What we do know, however, is the summit leaders' band-aid therapy of creating consistent warning labels, PACs, mentoring programs, and think tanks are safe, feel-good initiatives that avoid the *real* issues of irresponsible influential lyrics and behavior.

Unfortunately, Simmons doesn't have exclusive rights on such manipulative tactics. His ploys to elude responsibility are mimicked and often surpassed by other industry diehards who help perpetuate hip-hop's downward spiral. Fortunately, once challenged, their arguments are revealed to be fraught with unstable foundations.

Argument 1:
Parents should be role models
for their children, not entertainers

When former NBA superstar Charles Barkley declared that he was not a role model he spurred a groundswell of support from other public figures who shunned the noble task of behaving responsibly. This phenomenon of celebrities denouncing the notion of walking a straight line for the betterment of their impressionable fans has overwhelmingly permeated the hip-hop industry.

The mistake, however, in Barkley's proclamation is that it presumes people have the choice of determining whether they are role models. Like your race, the precious honor of being a role model is bestowed upon you beyond your control.

Barkley's problem isn't that he's a role model—it's that he's not a *good* role model. And by professing not to be examples for impressionable hip-hop fans, rappers erroneously believe they are exempt from behaving responsibly. As a result, they often misguide the people who revere them.

In defense of this theory, entertainers often attempt to relieve themselves of any social accountability by delegating role-model responsibilities to parents. Their rationale is that the leading influence in a child's life should be the people who rear them. While theoretically this premise could ultimately reroute the course of the nation if successful, it doesn't consider the reality of modern-day childbearing and mass marketing.

Consider the popular African proverb, used by Hillary Rodham Clinton in a community values campaign, "It takes a village to raise a child." The author of that nugget of wisdom understood two truths concerning children.

The first truth is that children aren't stationary beings who sit idly by, waiting for their parents to instruct them. Children, instead, are active people who often stumble into mischief away from their parents while roaming their neighborhoods, schools, and churches. To limit the chances of their youthful urges and inclinations leading them astray, the wisdom of mature neighbors, teachers, friends, family members, and role models is necessary to instruct children in the absence of their primary caretakers.

With unprecedented access to transportation, skyrocketing youth involvement in organized recreational activities outside the home, and a sobering number of excessively worked single parents, this African proverb should resonate with Americans more today than ever. But sadly, in today's world of decreased hands-on parenting, this philosophy often takes a backseat to more reclusive rearing techniques.

The second truth is that children are multifaceted individuals who require many diverse people to cater to their various curiosities and multiple interests, which ultimately mature them into well-rounded adults. Rarely does a single family harbor all the necessary personalities, talents, knowledge, spiritual depth, and life experience to fully satisfy a child. To complete the child's development, the *village* must participate in the rearing process by providing social, educational, spiritual, and recreational supplements.

Entertainers who insist that parents serve as lead role models to their children have a commendable perception of how the family and social structure should operate. They believe that children should revere the people who care for them by going to work every day, paying the bills, putting food in their stomachs, and providing guidance.

As practical as this philosophy sounds, it doesn't consider the antagonistic realities that offset it. Certainly, a parent should be the most influential person in a child's life, but the glitzy, multimillion-dollar, mass-marketed image campaigns to promote the latest hip-hop artist make it difficult for no-frills, old-school disciplinarians to compete.

It's much easier for children to find solace in a distant hip-hop icon who touts a message that "parents just don't understand" than in a mom and dad who punish them for making bad grades, forgetting to take out the garbage, or coming in after hours. Parents in these instances become the villains, while the artists (who have no hands-on responsibility in raising the child) become heroes.

Interestingly enough, the nation was blindsided several years ago by a purple dinosaur named Barney that captured the hearts and undying attention of a legion of young children. During that time, several celebrities confessed that their children would rather watch videos of a singing extinct mammal rather than celebrate their celebrity status. That means the celebrities' influence on their children was potentially compromised by the likes of a rhythmical Tyrannosaurus Rex.

Multiply the intensity of Barney's influence on children by the number of mass-marketed messages of sex, violence, drugs, alcohol, misogyny, and overindulgences, and it becomes quite clear why the hip-hop generation is in desperate need of role models inside and outside of the home. The overwhelming presence of deplorable hip-hop icons with strongholds on the world's youth gives just cause for all those concerned with the future to serve as their brother's keeper.

Several decades prior to the hip-hop revolution, the Rev. Dr. Martin Luther King Jr. prophesized the danger in this philosophy of limited accountability. "The world in which we live demands that we transform this worldwide neighborhood into a worldwide brotherhood," he explained. "Together we must learn to live as brothers, or together we will be forced to perish as fools."

Dr. King was right. The call for brotherhood in the hip-hop community rings louder than ever. How will the icons and power figures answer?

Argument 2:
Our lyrics aren't for kids

Many hip-hop artists claim that they don't make their lyrics for children but probably can't fathom the thought of building a lucrative career without support from the millions of young, influential fans who finance their music. According to Recording Industry Association of America statistics, the ten- to twenty-four-year-old demographic purchases approximately 35 percent of the music sold in America. So artists' statistical chances of reaching even a modicum of success is limited if they don't capture the ear of America's youth.

The marketing strategies that expose artists to their potential buying audiences contradict the assertion that hip-hop lyrics aren't made with children in mind. For instance, two of the grandest platforms for hip-hop artists to promote their work are MTV's *Total Request Live* and BET's *106 & Park*. Both shows feature a daily music video countdown, celebrity guest appearances, live interviews, and strategically air in the afternoon when school is out. But the main ingredients of both shows are the rambunctious, adolescent audience participants who offer their critiques of new videos and ask questions of their favorite artists. Though these artists argue their lyrics are for adults, it is no coincidence that they make appearances and debut their videos on shows where programmers work hard to create youthful formats.

This weak argument assumes that its opposition won't recognize the purchasing strength of the teenagers and young adults who underwrite hip-hop. But few of these opponents could fathom what would happen if adolescents stopped purchasing "adult hip-hop." Would the artists change their messages to meet the demands of the remaining adult audience, or would they hold fast to their need to speak candidly about sex, drugs, violence, and overindulgences? It's safe to assume

45

that thug rap would live no more under either circumstance. In short, the meal ticket for thug artists *does* rest in the wallets of hip-hop's impressionable youth.

Argument 3:
Freedom of speech

For centuries, it has served as a liberal posturing platform. It has granted legal immunity to what some consider the most unpardonable messages. It has helped divide races, neighborhoods, and even a country. And as expected, the great divider known as the First Amendment has found favor among many hip-hop guardians who use it to defend questionable rap lyrics.

Ratified December 15, 1791, the First Amendment reads:

> *"Congress shall make no law respecting an establishment of religion, or prohibiting the free exercise thereof; or abridging the freedom of speech, or of the press; or the right of the people peaceably to assemble, and to petition the Government for a redress of grievances."*

Arguments on behalf of these constitutional rights have fueled many liberal freedom-of-speech campaigns in the hip-hop industry. Most notable were the very public debates over the abrasive lyrics of 2 Live Crew and Ice-T. In 1990, members of 2 Live Crew — infamous for its preoccupation with crude sexual lyrics—were arrested for performing obscene material in a Florida nightclub. The controversy surrounding the arrests provoked emotionally charged comments from people representing both aspects of the debate and the group's popular protest record, "Banned in the U.S. A.," a spin-off of rock-n-roll icon Bruce Springsteen's most famous song, "Born in the U.S.A."

In "Banned in the U.S.A.," group leader Luther Campbell charged:

This is America.
We have the right to say what we want to say.
We have the right to do what we want to do.
And what I do in my house, you might not do in your house.
So what I do in my house is my business.
And the simple fact of it all is that we are bonded by the First Amendment.
We have the freedom of expression.
We have the freedom of choice.
And you--Chinese, Black, Green, Purple, Jew--
You have the right to listen to whoever you want to-
Even the 2 Live Crew.

Ice-T garnered national attention in 1992 for the song "Cop Killer" in which he and his band Body Count encouraged listeners to "bust some shots off" and "dust some cops off." The song made the former street hustler and the Time-Warner media conglomerate subjects of national protests by police, politicians, and concerned citizens who believed the rapper and the record label had crossed a thick line of decency.

In defense of its artist, Time-Warner issued a statement that read, "It is vital that we stand by our commitment to the free expression of ideas for all our authors, journalists, recording artists, screenwriters, actors, and directors."

In both instances, the defense for these artists hid behind the right to free speech. The rush to embrace the liberties of the constitutional amendments supports the claim that free-speech zealots have few, if any, substantial debates of merit to support the necessity of mass-marketed vulgar, violent, and vile lyrics. This one-dimensional stance often loses steam when removed from the scope of censorship and challenged in the broader spectrum of social responsibility.

After the attacks on September 11, 2001, journalists scattered to procure any information they could to inform the nation about America's war on terrorism. In fierce battles to scoop one another and enlighten their audiences, journalists began to inundate the airwaves and newspapers with information that compromised the safety of the nation. Vulnerable security procedures at airports and weak links in major water filtration systems, which were thought to be targets for biotech attacks, were exposed in lead stories all across the country.

In an attempt to curb the dissemination of information that increased the nation's susceptibility to more attacks, many concerned citizens, politicians, and even media types pleaded with journalists to withhold compromising information. They knew that the continued profiling of our nation's weak points would ultimately render us even more vulnerable. Therefore, it was widely understood that what they sought from the reporters was not censorship but a higher calling of responsible reporting.

Similarly, many parents and concerned citizens recognize that the harmful lyrics of some hip-hop artists compromise the safety and potential of their impressionable listeners. To little avail, these proponents have pleaded for rappers to act more responsibly in their capacity as mass-marketed role models by toning down their abrasive and misguided messages. Unfortunately, these pleas for responsible entertainment are too often met with unfavorable responses that ultimately return to a debate over civil liberties.

As a result, individuals who are extended rights without adhering to any responsibilities become examples of abused authority, insensitive and immature behavior, and one-dimensional agendas.

Consider the teenagers who are given the liberty to drive their parents' cars. The gift to drive creates an appreciated freedom to travel. However, if that freedom isn't balanced with the responsibility of coming home at a reasonable hour, filling the tank, and driving within the legal limits it is considered an abused privilege.

Conscienceless hip-hop entertainers have abused America's unique privilege of free speech by failing to fill up the near-empty tank of morality that plagues the genre, rarely responding proactively to the misfortunes of the susceptible listeners they lead astray, and too often succumbing to the penalties of unlawful behavior.

Like Luther Campbell, many entertainers erroneously believe the First Amendment grants them unequivocal immunity from the long arm of the law. For those who believe that free speech is a carte-blanche privilege to say anything anywhere, try walking through the entrance of any American airport and jokingly screaming, "I have a gun!" Although we as Americans have the freedom of expression and the right to bear arms, you would undoubtedly find yourself behind bars with a fine waiting for you after your release. Yes, free-speech privileges actually come at a price.

One might argue, then, that the First Amendment is falsely advertised because in these instances it obviously isn't free. That's because the forefathers who wrote it intended to offer peace of mind to those who wished to openly express their religious beliefs and personal philosophies and question our democratic government. They didn't write the First Amendment to allow irresponsible trumpeters to jeopardize the safety of innocent people.

The intent of those who call for more responsible entertainment is not necessarily to censor artists; but more importantly to protect the fans that they influence. They fear too many artist-fan relationships will mimic the one featured on the introduction to Tupac's song "Outlaw":

Tupac: That's right, nigga. You gotta get your papers in this muthafucker. I ain't mad at you at all. What the fuck you want to be when you grow up, Ra Ra?

Ra Ra: Nigga, is you stupid? I want to be a muthafucking outlaw!

Tupac: That's right, nigga. Ha, ha. Housing these hoes. You feel me? You got to be that shit. You keeping it real, nigga, or what?

Ra Ra: I'm keeping it real!

Tupac: How old are you, nigga?

Ra Ra: I'm 11.

Because saying the wrong thing at the wrong place and time can be dangerous to innocent people, it's only a matter of time before the free speech privileges granted to artists are re-evaluated. Artists increasingly jeopardize the safety and potential of their impressionable listeners through their irresponsible lyrics. Their cries of free speech and censorship will eventually lose steam in a society that is beginning to understand the wisdom in Dr. King's words: "A true revolution of value will soon cause us to question the fairness and justice of many of our past and present policies."

Wise industry insiders who have seen the writing on the wall have been behooved to take precautions (although quite limited) to offset predictable attacks by organizations like the

National Parent Teacher Association and the Parents' Music Resource Center.

In 1985, the RIAA agreed to place "Explicit Lyrics" warning labels on music with questionable content. Initially, it seemed a noble gesture on behalf of the music industry to "balance an artist's right of self-expression with parents' need for information to make choices based on their children's individual situation and their own values." However, the realization that many young people purchase music apart from their parents altered the labels' perceived effectiveness.

When parents learned that their children were permitted to purchase profane music without their consent it ruined the legitimacy of a potential revolutionary idea. And the stance by RIAA to maintain the status quo helped further divide liberals and conservatives on the issue.

During a 2001 Congressional hearing, RIAA president and CEO Hilary B. Rosen explained, "Our label is an advisory logo about explicit lyrics. It makes no judgments—nor do we think such judgments are warranted or possible—about what is appropriate for any specific age group."

With its stance, the RIAA alienated itself from other industries that have deemed its potentially harmful products off-limits to underage consumers. It is illegal, for instance, for minors to purchase, rent, or participate in any pornographic material. And people under the age of twenty-one are prohibited from purchasing or drinking any form of alcohol.

However, despite the recording industry's enormous capacity to negatively impact youthful listeners, Rosen and other industry executives find it unnecessary to establish boundaries for susceptible music fans. They argue that boundaries are neither warranted nor possible to establish because fans' maturity level runs the gamut. Obviously they chose not to benchmark the alcohol industry, which prohibits sales to anyone under the age of twenty-one no matter their tolerance level for alcohol. The liquor industry's "better safe than sorry" policy is one from which the record industry could definitely learn.

Argument 4:
Rappers are merely street reporters for the hood

In the movie *Boyz N the Hood*, Doughboy (played by rapper Ice Cube) tried to explain why his brother's violent murder wasn't reported on the news. "Either they don't know, don't show, or don't care about what's going on in the hood," he exclaimed.

Doughboy's sentiments capture the feelings of many African Americans who have struggled to understand why news in their neighborhoods is often underreported or unreported. For decades, their cries for balanced, fair reporting fell on deaf ears and prompted rappers to fill the void by rhythmically telling the untold stories of their communities.

The immense popularity of hip-hop music in today's culture legitimizes the claim that there is a great demand for urban-related broadcasts. Even more, this cultural phenomenon has given new meaning to the term "street reporter." However, if rap music is now "black America's CNN," as rapper Chuck D claims, its journalists are characteristically more biased than professional reporters who often eliminate the African American perspective from their broadcasts and stories.

With fixed, mass-marketed messages of buffoonery, hip-hop artists are too often guilty of perpetuating the same negative urban stereotypes as professional reporters who turn to the nearest forty-ounce-drinking, shower-cap-wearing, gold-tooth-smiling, English-is-a-second-language person for a sound bite on the eleven o'clock news. Consider, for instance, some of the top hip-hop songs of 2002:

"Roll Out" (Ludacris): Glorifies gun use

"We Thuggin'" (Fat Joe featuring R. Kelly): Self-explanatory

"Lights, Camera, Action!" (Mr. Cheeks): An ode to strippers

"Bouncin' Back" (Mystikal): A music video about a hospitalized lunatic

"Feelin' On Yo' Booty" (R. Kelly): Self-explanatory

If the characteristics of these songs were personified in an individual selected to give an account of his community, concern would arise about his ability to accurately represent a multidimensional neighborhood. Yet, when hip-hop entertainers who claim to be "street reporters" package their accounts of the "hood" in misrepresenting tales of pimps, gangs, drug dealers, alcoholics, and nymphomaniacs, they are accepted as the voice of balance for their communities.

But just like the professional reporters who perpetually ignore or misrepresent the ghetto, many hip-hop entertainers ascribe to a similarly unbalanced practice of glorifying the worst of the culture. They rarely disclose tales about the intelligent hip-hop diehard who manages to avoid drugs, abstain from alcohol, obtain a college degree, penetrate the ranks of corporate America, wear more gold on his wedding ring finger than his teeth, and go to church every Sunday. And if they do decide to tell such a story it's usually buried deep in their albums and rarely mass-marketed. In an attempt to balance the lack of news coverage about their communities, many hip-hop artists have tried to make a right with two wrongs by committing the same journalistic crime as professional reporters.

In essence, the characteristics of hip-hop street reporters and professional journalists who misrepresent the ghetto are not much different. Both can argue that their "reports" are not solely thug accounts, yet rarely do their positive messages of the ghetto lead off news broadcasts or help launch marketing campaigns for albums. Both are guilty of building reputations by profiling the worst of the ghetto. And by avoiding the community's positive aspects they prove they either don't know, don't show, or don't care about what's *really* going on in the hood.

Argument 5:
Don't judge me

An unwritten rule in the entertainment industry states: "Thou shall not judge." This rule prohibits any entertainment insider or zealot to accept cross-judgment from outsiders who recognize improprieties in artists' work.

This judgment moratorium typically rears its head in the midst of harsh criticism and often accomplishes its goal of avoiding condemnation by establishing impervious creative boundaries for artists.

Grammy winner Missy Elliott, known for sometimes straddling the fence of brilliant creativity and salacious tactlessness, sought refuge from the unfavorable criticism of her naysayers in her gospel-esque song "I'm Moving On":

> *A lot of people are quick to criticize me for the kind of music I sing,*
> *But see they don't change the belief that I have in God.*
> *Please don't judge me cause I'm not perfect.*
> *And please don't judge me if I'm not in church on Sunday.*
> *I'm moving on.*

During a televised verbal exchange with hip-hop historian Kevin Powell about the influence of Tupac, Suge

Knight, the artist's former manager, used this judgment philosophy to defend the slain rapper.

> **Powell:** Are we going to look at the positive stuff of his life and try to learn from it, which is that this brother was trying to be a leader for his community? Or are we going to look at the negative stuff, which I think is also important to look at, like this is some of the stuff that black men should *not* get into—the excessive drinking, the excessive smoking, the materialism?
>
> **Knight:** Oh, so now you're going to judge him?

(Coincidentally, Tupac wrote a song called "Only God Can Judge Me Now" before his death in 1996.)

The "judgment card" that hip-hop aficionados often play when their backs are against the wall of criticism creates a dangerous double standard by only welcoming the favorable opinions of critics. The intent of this reputation management tactic is to leave no room for public scrutiny while clearing the way for public praise.

Consider the awards Elliott has received for her music from entities like The Source, the National Academy of Recording Arts and Sciences, and Billboard. Instead of pleading for these nomination committees not to pass judgment on her work, she instead graciously accepted these awards that were predicated on the ability to judge her music along with many other artists. The qualifying difference is that her work is favorably critiqued in a glamorous fashion and not scrutinized in a way that makes her susceptible to public moral inspection.

Unfortunately, this judgment tactic suggests that no one can flip the coin and evaluate the other side of artists' work. As outsiders, it simply relegates us to admiring the ability of an artist to make our heads bob and nothing more. But a true exploration of artists' work can only occur with a balanced opportunity to dissect its good, bad, and ugly characteristics.

Argument 6:
If you don't like it, don't buy it

According to super producer Dr. Dre, there was only one alternative for those who took odds with the music he made as a member of the now-defunct group N.W.A. (Niggas With Attitude). "We didn't care what people said," he admitted. "If you don't like, don't buy it."

Dr. Dre and many others mistakenly believe the practical solution to quieting those who take issue with hip-hop's dark side is to suggest that they turn a deaf ear to the culture. The reality is that hip-hop artists aren't selling many albums to their critics to begin with, which thwarts the effectiveness of this recommendation.

With a few exceptions, hip-hop's critics rarely purchase the music, watch the videos or closely monitor the industry, yet because of its ubiquitous presence, they find themselves surrounded by the culture that hip-hop creates.

Those critics are similar to the sorority girl who went to a college keg party. Although she refrained from drinking, she couldn't avoid the intoxicated fraternity boys who persistently approached her to make unflattering gestures. After deciding to escape the rowdy venue, she was killed in a car accident by a drunk driver who was returning to the party after making a beer run. Although she didn't indulge in the plentiful amount of alcohol available at the party, she still suffered from the effects it had on those around her.

Similarly, hip-hop's critics understand that they don't have to be tuned into the culture to feel its effects. They know that even if they avoid listening to hip-hop music, watching hip-hop videos, reading hip-hop magazines, or wearing hip-hop clothes they're still susceptible to the unflattering attitudes, violent behavior, dangerous sexual agendas, and lewd behavior of some of those who indulge in the culture.

Many of them are rightfully concerned that although they could conceivably eliminate hip-hop from their children's cultural diet, they can't guarantee that their daughters won't be the victim of some Ja Rule fan who emulates the rapper's lyrics: "I got girls all across the sea, and I keep 'em drugged up off that Ecstasy."

According to the "if you don't like it, don't buy it" philosophy, the only tactic critics can employ to address their issues with hip-hop is to avoid it. However, wise critics know that the destinies of hip-hop fans and haters are inextricably linked. They know that avoiding the commotion in the hip-hop industry is like a first-class passenger ignoring the ruckus in the back of an airplane. Although the immediate threat isn't in first class, passengers understand that if the people in the coach section cause the airplane to go down, they go down with it. Therefore, it behooves them to restore order in the back of the airplane, like it does critics to improve the hip-hop industry to ensure safety in every community

Argument 7:
We're just giving the people what they want

Another empty argument used in attempts to justify the questionable messages disseminated through hip-hop contends artists are simply giving fans what they want. They claim that their messages of irresponsible sex, overindulgence in alcohol and material goods, drug use, violence, and misogyny are merely responses to the demands of the market.

This rationale implicitly suggests that when the fans decide they want to see and hear something different, the industry will give them something different. Even more, it attempts to shift the blame for the troubled state of the industry into the hands of the fans and allow entertainment profiteers to pursue their single-minded capitalist agendas with no conscience.

Those who understand the laws of economics know there is a certain amount of legitimacy to this philosophy of giving consumers what they want. The organizers of the Civil Rights movement proved they understood it when they implemented Operation Breadbasket in the 1960s. Through their plan, activists orchestrated boycotts to financially cripple companies that exploited the African American community. After successfully boycotting, they were able to persuade stubborn company executives to alter their business plans to include the wants and needs of African Americans.

In a similar fashion, a tremendous amount of power exists within the entertainment consumer markets to wield significant change throughout the industry. Surely if the millions of fans who purchase hip-hop products suddenly demanded that the industry create more socially-responsible products or risk losing billions of dollars, hip-hop would take on a new agenda.

Unfortunately, launching such a boycott among hip-hop fans is a more daunting task today than it was for deprived blacks during the Civil Rights movement. The very record labels, artists, and icons that stand in the way of creating a better hip-hop industry are the same ones that capture the attention of fans with multimillion-dollar thug campaigns that flood radio stations, television shows, magazines, and Internet sites.

The appeal of those campaigns is so great that they put the absorbed hip-hop fan in the same dilemma to boycott artists as it does a drug addict to boycott his supplier. No addict who receives conscienceless satisfaction from the drugs provided by his dealer will boycott the source of his happiness. Nor are hip-hop fans likely to turn their backs on the artists they cheer.

Therefore, it becomes hypocritical for hip-hop artists to say they're only giving fans what they want, when, in fact, their promotional machines helped create the fans' need. That argument is as self-serving as a drug dealer who helps to hook someone on dope and then grandstands that he's simply giving the drug addict what he wants. So it's not very likely that hip-hop thug dealers will ever hear their addicted fans ask for anything more than the unbalanced drivel they produce until the industry leaders decide to offer them something more or completely cut them off.

Unfortunately, there are only three hopes for the drug addict and hip-hop thug addict to escape the imminent dangers associated with their addictions. First, the addict must realize the threats their obsession poses and launch a self-imposed effort to kick the habit. Their second hope is to have a concerned individual intervene on his behalf and initiate a rehabilitation process. The third hope is for the addict's dealers to refuse to continue contributing to his demise and cut off his supply.

Although the need for self-improvement and the intervention of loved ones are the most common routes taken to break the bondage of addiction, there must be an increased awakening among the dealers for addicts to thoroughly overcome their strongholds. If not, many millions of lives will be continually jeopardized by an attitude that unjustifiably caters to the detrimental desires of society's vulnerable suspects.

This argument of "giving fans what they want" is more simply countered in the framework of parenthood. If little Johnny asks for a cookie prior to dinner, parents who understand the importance of good eating habits and reserving appetites won't give him the treat simply because that's what he wants. Instead, they deny him the pleasure of the cookie because they know that it will adversely affect the eating habits and appetite they were trying to protect.

But because hip-hop has given too many little Johnnies their proverbial cookies before dinnertime, it has ruined their appetites for self-respect and social responsibility and subsequently created a generation of Johnny-come-latelys who take pleasure in drug use, promiscuous sex, and hedonistic pleasures.

Argument 8:
Our lyrics don't affect listeners

In his autobiography Russell Simmons contends, "Despite what those outside the culture think, regular hip-hop buyers aren't idiots who turn on the radio, hear a few words, and then run out and do what the records say."

As a fledgling producer and manager in the mid-1980s, however, Simmons helped make Run-D.M.C.'s song "My Adidas" a hit and subsequently convinced Adidas executives to give the group a $5 million promotion deal based on a 30 percent hike in sneaker sales after the release of the song. Undoubtedly, the deal with Adidas would not have materialized without Simmons' ability to convince the sports apparel company that Run-D.M.C.'s pronounced admiration for its shoes influenced fans' purchasing decisions. (I sure bought a pair.)

Rarely, if ever, does this feeble argument that lyrics don't affect hip-hop listeners hold water. It's fraught with far too many hypocritical actions on the part of the artists and executives like Simmons, who attempt to pass it off as an uncompromised doctrine.

For example, why would hip-hop artists waste time on socially redemptive songs like "Self Destruction" and "We're All in the Same Gang," which were made to curb violence in the hip-hop community, if they didn't believe their lyrical contributions could make a difference? Or why would some of the most popular young artists join forces for the post-September 11 song "What's Going On" to promote world peace if they believed their efforts would be made in vain? They wouldn't! These projects offer artists admirable opportunities to use their lyrical influence to promote respectable causes.

Unfortunately, many of them won't agree that the same influence they use to promote peace can be used to incite ill will. Their contradicting comments and actions create a dangerous double standard that says lyrics can only influence avid listeners when they're used for good but irresponsible messages bear no consequence.

And as if debating with entertainers isn't enough, this battle to prove that lyrics can be harmful might be easier fought if misled fans weren't so quick to chime in. Many of them believe that listening to absorbent amounts of thug music will not produce adverse affects. They listen to one polluted message after another with an ironman complex that suggests they have the unwavering capacity to decide how those lyrics will or won't influence their behavior.

Even without the support of scientific studies or religious doctrine that indicate listening, reading, and viewing habits can influence behavior, a compelling rebuttal is offered in a story told by the Rev. Mason Betha of a young boy who's seen too many salacious hip-hop videos.

"There was a little boy who flipped out at a photo shoot," Betha said as he remembered his time as a rap star. "He took off all of his clothes and started masturbating right there at the shoot. He was like twelve years old. He just flipped out.

"That's crazy. You can't stay around the devil's work and say it won't affect you," he declared. "You can't lay in pig's slop and think you're clean."

4

F--- THE WORLD

"Hated for the cussing,
but the hatred made us cuss more."
— Nappy Roots
"Awnaw"

The 1992 movie *Juice* was an underground hit that featured rising stars Tupac Shakur, Jermaine Hopkins, Khalil Kain, and Omar Epps. In the movie, the four play a tight-knit high school posse that cut class together, fight neighborhood bullies, and plan the robbery of a neighborhood convenient store. After the robbery goes terribly awry, Tupac's character, Bishop, inadvertently kills one of the members of the clique in a tussle for the pistol used in the holdup.

Bishop's relationship with his two remaining friends quickly dissolves as he attempts to wield unreasonable authority over them with an amateurish scheme to cover the murder. The climax of the movie is preceded by a confrontational face-off between Bishop and Epps' character, Q:

Q: You crazy, man.

Bishop: You know what, when you said that last time, I was
kind of trippin', right? But now, you're right. I am
crazy. But you know what else? I don't give a fuck. I
don't give a fuck about you! I don't give a fuck about
Steel! And I don't give a fuck about Raheem either! I
don't give a fuck about myself! Look, I ain't shit! I
ain't never gon' be shit! And you less of a man than
me so soon as I decide that you ain't gon' be shit,
POW! So be it! You remember that, muthafucker!
Cause I'm the one ya'll need to be worried about!

Those lines, which Tupac convincingly delivered more
than a decade ago, encapsulate the sentiments of a new
generation of hip-hop proponents who have developed a strong
contempt for the traditional values of their parents and
grandparents. Instead of embracing messages typically
considered pure, holy, decent, and wholesome, hip-hop's new
generation chooses to glorify society's ugly underbelly and its
propensity for evil, vile, insensitive, and degrading behavior.
Their sordid artistic bellows, which mimic Bishop's "I don't give
a f---" attitude, have managed to transcend nearly every facet of
hip-hop.

"There is no question in my mind that young people
today have hit an all-time low relative to respectability," said Joe
Clark, the former principal of New Jersey's Eastside High
depicted in the movie *Lean On Me*. "They don't respect their
mothers or fathers. They don't respect senior citizens or teachers,
and a great wrath is thrown at law enforcement officers. We are

67

headed for a rendezvous with something tragic." Clark is now
director of the Essex County Juvenile Center in Newark, N.J.

The disdainful actions of morally corrupt hip-hop artists
and the tactics employed by proponents have created a societal
vacuum that wantonly attempts to suck out the purities in
popular culture. If society says go right, hip-hop goes left.
Instead of life, hip-hop chooses death. Instead of praying to
heaven, hip-hop fantasizes about hell. Instead of practicing
abstinence, hip-hop promotes promiscuity. Instead of finding
safety in moderation, hip-hop walks the dangerous tightrope of
excess. And instead of choosing to "just say no," hip-hop decides
to stay "high 'til I die."

Proof of the culture's current decline in values requires
little investigative effort. A person need only examine the names
of some of the genre's record companies to learn how well its
contemptuous agendas have been institutionalized. Labels like
Bad Boy Entertainment, Death Row, Murder Inc., Ruthless, and
Aftermath tell the story. Complementing the rebellious labels are
scornfully named artists such as Kurupt, Gang Starr, Niggas
With Attitude, Bytches Wit Problems, Compton's Most Wanted,
Naughty By Nature, The Alkaholiks, Ghostface Killer, and
Junior M.A.F.I.A., to name a few.

If, like Shakespeare, you question the ability of a
moniker to accurately define someone and ask, "What's in a
name?" the artists' subject matter surely reveals their
contemptuous intent. Songs like "Pimp Juice" (Nelly), "Fuck The

World" (Tupac), "Pocket Full Of Stones" (UGK), and "Kill You" (Eminem) characterize the moral constitution of many high-profile artists.

The disdainful overtones in songs like these have emerged as the prevailing marketing attractions for hip-hop profiteers. The contemptuous appeal has become so lucrative that African American record executives Russell Simmons and Luther Campbell chose to play the race card in efforts to convince critics not to deny them the same right to market their desecrating acts as afforded white smut panderers.

At a 2001 hearing of the U.S. Committee on Government Affairs, Simmons expressed concern about a Federal Trade Commission study on explicit lyrics in music. The study profiled 29 songs with explicit lyrics, 22 of which were hip-hop songs performed by African American artists.

During the hearing, Simmons shared his views on the study with the committee by saying, "My final point is that it is often largely about race. And it makes some of us very concerned that few publicly admit that this effort to censure hip-hop has deep-seated racial overtones."

He went on to add, "The Federal Trade Commission's report on explicit content disproportionately focused on black hip-hop artists."

And to explain why he believed his rap group was the focus of high-profile controversy while other equally raunchy acts were overlooked, 2 Live Crew's Campbell told *USA Today*,

"I know that in the world today there are a lot of people who just don't want to see a young black man succeed."

In an amazing reversal of racial struggles, Simmons and Campbell sought to leverage their ethnicity to recoup privileges members of the Civil Rights movement detested. In the 1960s, Dr. King, the Freedom Fighters, and others fought so that blacks could have the opportunity to rise and compete on the same level as America's best white citizens. Conversely, Simmons, Campbell, and other hip-hop advocates are currently fighting to have their standards lowered so they can compete with the worst of white America.

Sadly, they now want to fight for the right to be more like Ozzy Osbourne. When Pepsi decided to end its advertising relationship with rapper Ludacris because of his X-rated lyrics yet paraded the foul-mouthed Osbourne family as its new marketing icon during the 2003 Super Bowl the powers-that-be in the hip-hop community went hysterical. Some went as far as to threaten a boycott against the soft-drink giant because of its decision to choose a white bad boy representative rather than a black one.

A simple example of school discipline might better explain hip-hop's direction. An elementary school teacher with a class full of misbehaved children called the parents of her lone African American student to inform them of their child's behavior. Upon learning that the teacher had not called the parents of the other students, the African American parents adopted a Russell Simmons- and Luther Campbell-like mindset. Instead of welcoming the opportunity to improve their child's behavior, they complained that little Johnny was singled out.

For equality sake, the African American parents thought it was more important to ensure their child was granted the same undisciplined opportunity to "act a fool" as the white children. They completely overlooked their accountability in ensuring their child doesn't become a victim of his own detrimental behavior—even if it means he'll be the only properly behaved student in the class.

Many hip-hop executives have assumed the role of the parents in this story and have too often screamed "racism" when they should have gone to the proverbial tool shed to "straighten out" their "children" (i.e. artists). Even if their cries of racism are true, it still doesn't deny the fact that there are legitimate issues with the messages in their songs that are indifferent to bigotry.

Solving racism won't solve the problems in their music or the behavior of a delinquent child. If racism has a positive attribute, it could be that it creates an advantage for those who rise to the challenge of perfection set by racists. When a racist singles out an African American student or hip-hop artist for their misconduct, it should challenge that person to take an introspective look at himself and make wholesale improvements. Such introspection ultimately casts a person as a better artist and/or student than his counterparts.

Unfortunately, controversial hip-hop executives typically avoid these suggested accountability practices and opt for strategies that allow them to continue misbehaving. After sharing his thoughts with the Senate committee about entertainment rating systems, Simmons practiced this theory by submitting an editorial to the New York Times.

"I am proud to say that when I stood up in the Senate, I upheld the traditions of hip-hop, being a little bit rude for the sake of speaking the truth," Simmons wrote. "But I also acted to protect the rights of all Americans. If the government can target African American artists for censorship, no one's freedom of expression is safe."

There's no denying that America's intrigue with roughneck characters who play by their own rules existed long before hip-hop emerged as a dominant culture. In fact, one of the most revered rebels in American history is 1950s actor James Dean. Long before Sean "P. Diddy" Combs glamorized life as a bad boy, Dean captured the hearts of America's youth with his performance in the classic movie *Rebel Without A Cause*. Even after his untimely death at the age of 24 with only three movies to his credit, Dean's fans maintained a long-lasting adoration for his rebellious tendencies both on and off the screen.

Dean biographer Joe Hyams endeavored to explain the appeal of the timeless rebel. "There is no simple explanation for why he has come to mean so much to so many people today," he wrote. "Perhaps it is because, in his acting, he had the intuitive talent for expressing the hopes and fears that are part of all young people. In some movie magic way, he managed to dramatize brilliantly the questions every young person in every generation must resolve."

Despite Dean's great acting ability, it wasn't his thespian skills alone that helped him capture young America's attention. For repressed adolescents, his renditions of the unleashed rebel provide a vicarious outlet, offering hope that they too might escape the confines of their situations.

In *Juice*, Tupac's character Bishop raves about James Cagney's 1949 performance as a kamikaze outlaw in the movie *White Heat*. Cagney's character dies in a dramatic battle with police, to which Bishop pronounced, "If you gotta go out, that's how you go out. That muthafucker took his destiny in his own hands!"

While the gangster craze does predate hip-hop, it's painfully obvious that the phenomenon serves as a leading inspiration for the culture. The current infatuation with gangster life can be traced to more recent flicks like *The Godfather* series, *Good Fellas*, and *New Jack City*, which serve as celebrated blueprints for those intrigued with hardcore insurgency.

Rapper Jay-Z used memorable scenes from the movies *Scarface* and *Carlito's Way* as backdrops to his first two albums. The violence, drugs, and greed profiled in both movies helped provide much of the content for Jay-Z's "Reasonable Doubt" and "In My Lifetime, Vol. 1," which are considered classic albums in many hip-hop circles. And award-winning rapper Scarface (formerly of The Geto Boys) was so impressed with Al Pacino's performance that he assumed the stage name of the drug-dealing murderer.

So any accusations that hip-hop is responsible for society's current interest in gangster tales are completely inaccurate. Hip-hop, however, can be accurately accused of glorifying society's ugly underbelly with unprecedented fervor. No other generation or industry has contributed more collective resources in such a short amount of time to successfully promote abrasive, unhealthy, and immoral behavior and images.

Instead of relying solely on their personal hardships to market hip-hop's scornful agendas, many performers have solicited hardcore tales from past generations. Without hip-hop's contemptuous platform, most fans, particularly the new generation, would not be aware of dated names like Dolemite, Foxy Brown, Superfly, The Mack, Street Players, and Iceberg Slim. Once archived after the blaxploitation era, these movies, books, and artists were dusted off to provide hip-hop artists supplemental gangster material to legitimize their cause.

The constant showering of rebellious messages in the hip-hop culture have so soiled the minds of its listeners that a counterculture has germinated. That counterculture adores rappers like Trick Daddy and his song "I'm A Thug," in which he expresses his fondness for the thug lifestyle and his unwillingness to turn from it. To disguise the morally polluted song, Trick Daddy solicited the voices of an innocent-sounding youth ensemble to sing the chorus:

> I don't know what this world's gonna bring
> But I know one thing that this is the life for me
> Baby, cause I'm a thug
> All day, every day
> Baby, cause I'm a thug
> Wouldn't change for the world
> Uh huh, cause I'm a thug
> That's right you heard
> Baby, cause I'm a thug
> Uh huh, oh yeah

Trick Daddy ensues with the following verse:

> I'm representing thug shit
> This who I roll with
> Watch them niggas that's gonna love this
> Niggas who out on bond
> On the run
> Got 10 years on parole
> Since you can't say it, dog, I'ma say it for ya'll
> Motherfuck the po-pos
> Fuck the judge and CEOs
> Fuck the DA and POs
> Fuck the family of the victim
> Witness that's snitchin'-ass hoes, nigga

Despite its venomous lyrics, the playful chorus sung by children made this song radio-friendly enough for programmers across the country to add to their daily play lists. This wolf-in-sheep's-clothing marketing tactic has exposed a great number of susceptible fans to detrimental lyrics that should be stamped with a "don't try this at home" disclaimer.

Instead, many urban radio stations perpetuate hip-hop's stifling tendencies by inundating the airwaves with songs similar to "I'm A Thug." Other chart-topping songs that fit this profile include "Hard Knock Life" and "IZZO (H.O.V.A.)" by Jay-Z, "Always on Time" by Ja Rule, and "Country Grammar" by Nelly.

Even more, in a telling scenario that reveals how deep this counterculture has permeated hip-hop circles, disc jockeys who once were solely criticized for spinning controversial headline-making records are now making headlines with their controversial behavior.

Radio personalities Star and Buc Wild, hosts of the WQHT Hot 97 morning hip-hop show in New York, stood in the crosshairs of public outrage and planned boycotts after making deeply insensitive references to hip-hop singer Aaliyah's death. The morning after the beloved singer died in an airplane crash, shock jock Star played an audio sound clip of a woman screaming while inside a crashing plane.

His crass attempt to comically showcase Aaliyah's death was followed by a personal disclaimer that he is "The Hater" and it is "his" show. In utter defiance to anyone who opposed his insensitivity — including co-host Miss Jones, who cursed at him on the air and left the show for the day — Star broadcasted the sound clip of the screaming woman several times more.

Hip-hop's gruesome counterculture has created a morbid and grossly premature fixation with death. At a time when former generations lived with an unreasonable sense of invincibility, the hip-hop generation has given an unusual amount of attention to death and the afterworld.

R&B hip-hop singer Jaheim contributed to the cause with his 2002 hit, in which he solicits one last sexual encounter with his woman by proposing, "Just in case I don't make it home tonight, let me make love to you for the last time, baby."

Never in hip-hop has this obsession with death reared itself more notably than in the lyrics and lives of the genre's two greatest icons. The Notorious B.I.G. and Tupac established lyrical legacies in part by regularly flirting with the topic in their music.

The Notorious B.I.G. was so bent on mortality that he named his two albums *Ready To Die* and *Life After Death*. And throughout his career, Tupac seemingly sought to exhaust the topic with songs like "How Long Will They Mourn Me," "If I Die

2night," "Death Around the Corner," "I Wonder if Heaven Got a Ghetto," and "Only Fear of Death."

Unfortunately, their lyrical fixations with death were met with onslaughts of gunfire from unidentified murderers who turned their studio narratives into prophecies. Biggie professed on his last album "You're Nobody 'Til Somebody Kills You." And Tupac, in his song "So Many Tears," asked, "Will I survive til the morning to see the sun? Please, Lord, forgive me for my sins, 'cause here I come."

Within six months of one another, Tupac and B.I.G. were gunned down in similar fashions, bringing an end to one of the most renowned eras in rap music. In addition to losing two of hip-hop's most gifted rap artists, their murders catapulted the industry's fascination with the concept of martyrdom to new heights. Surely before their murders, artists had flirted with the concept of death, but a blatant abandonment for the sanctity of life quickly ensued.

Evidence that hip-hop entertainers have become transfixed with the idea of becoming martyrs can be found in the following song and album titles:

> **Pete Rock & CL Smooth** — "Death Becomes You"
> **Ice Cube** — "When I Get To Heaven," "When Will They Shoot"
> **Puff Daddy** — "Is This The End?," "If I Should Die Tonight"
> **Geto Boys** — "I Just Wanna Die"
> **Snoop Dogg** — "Murder Was The Case"
> **Slip Capone & CPO** — "The Eulogy"

DMX — "It's Dark and Hell is Hot," "24 Hours to Live," "It's Murda," "Why We Die," "Kiss of Death"
Ja Rule — "Kill 'em All," "Suicide Freestyle," "Murda For Life," "The Murders," "6 Feet Underground," "Dial M For Murder"
Jay-Z — "If I Should Die," "Ride or Die," "There's Been a Murder," "Squeeze 1st"
Master P — "Is There a Heaven for a Gangster?"
Mystikal — "Ain't Gonna See Tomorrow," "Murder III"
Nas — "Shoot 'em Up," "Last Words"

Because of songs like these, which are often accompanied by graphic videos, hip-hop's new generation believes it's a glorious feat to die young. Instead of planning a 401(k), the music and television they faithfully watch tell them death is a more imminent reality.

Catering to hip-hop's intrigue with death, *Vibe* magazine paid homage to dead hip-hop artists Troy "Trouble T-Roy" Dixon, 1968-1990; Latasha Rogers, a.k.a. MC Trouble, 1970-1991; Darren "Buffy" Robinson, a.k.a. the Human Beat Box, 1967-1995; Scott "DJ Scott La Rock" Sterling, 1962-1987; Raymond "Freaky Tah" Rogers, 1971-1999; Eric "Eazy-E" Wright, 1963-1995; Tupac Shakur, 1971-1996; Christopher Wallace, a.k.a. The Notorious B.I.G., 1972-1997; Keith "Cowboy" Wiggins, 1960-1989; Lamont "Big L" Coleman, 1973-1999; and Edward Seagram Miller, 1971-1996.

In that tribute, David Bry sought to explain their immortal status by writing: "Those artists, these artists — and there have doubtless been others — were taken from us, taken from where we stay, far too early. Taken by violence or illness or some fateful mishap. But they are still with us. In their words and songs, their souls preserved on record forever. They're still moving us. Still making us think and feel and shiver in awe of their spirit and of their gifts. And we can be thankful, at least, for that."

Despite the questionable circumstances surrounding some of their deaths, Bry attempted to tastefully describe the immortal status of these fallen hip-hop artists. And though Bry's eloquent words are appreciated by many, sometimes it takes the honesty of a social critic like Chris Rock to lend proper perspective to some of hip-hop's slain artists.

"I'm watching the news and they were like, 'Tupac Shakur was assassinated. Biggie Smalls was assassinated. Struck down by assassins bullets,'" Rock proclaimed. "And I'm like 'No, they wasn't!' Martin Luther King was assassinated. Malcolm X was assassinated. John F. Kennedy was assassinated. Them two niggas got shot! I love Tupac, I love Biggie, but school will be open on their birthday."

"I really have a difficult time with the music of today because I don't find it presentable. I don't find the young women being young women. I don't like all the flesh being shown. It would have been unacceptable when I was eighteen," said Grammy- and Emmy-winning vocalist Nancy Wilson. "I'm just concerned about how far we are going to go before we destroy what is good and right about us as a people. We need to bring a little class back to us as a people."

With more than fifty years as an entertainer, Wilson has seen firsthand the downward spiral of the industry. Like many, she is fed up with how it has shunned traditional values.

In her tirade she doesn't specify what spurred her disdain, but perhaps it was Eminem's preoccupation with glorified drug use, as illustrated in "I'm Shady":

> I think I got a generation brainwashed
> To pop pills and smoke pot till they brains rot
> Stop they blood flow until they veins clot
> I need a pain shot, and a shot of plain scotch
> Purple haze and acid raindrops

Or maybe it was the indiscretion of Lil Kim in her song "Magic Stick":

> I ain't out shopping spending dudes C-notes
> I'm in the crib giving niggaz deep throat
> Tonight Lil' Kim gon' have you in the zone
> Girls, call ya crib, I'm answering the phone
> Guys wanna wife me and give me the ring
> I'll do it anywhere, anyhow, I'm down for anything

Or maybe it was 50 Cent's blatant contempt for life as voiced in "Many Men (Wish Death)":

> *I put a hole in a nigga for fucking with me*
> *My back on the wall, now you gon' see*
> *Better watch how you talk, when you talk about me*
> *'Cause I'll come and take your life away*

Or maybe it was the irreverent lyrics of Keith Murray in "Get Lifted":

> *I do this for my niggas locked downed running capers*
> *Smoking herbs in the Bible papers*
> *But how does it feel when you got no fire*
> *And can't pass the dutchie* (marijuana cigarette) *on the left hand side*
> *What the fuck, who the fuck want to fuck with the six shot shooter*
> *I'll murder you over buddha* (weed)

Wilson's frustration with popular entertainment could have been prompted by its many indiscretions, but there's no denying that the industry she now despises is bent on the idea of pushing the "decency" envelope for the sake of "keeping it real." Today, with the help of multimillion-dollar marketing campaigns and an onslaught of thug messages, the crass images that once existed as "black sheep" in the industry are no longer anomalies. They are popular culture's prevailing influence.

Randall Kennedy, author of the book *nigger*, lends some perspective as to why the pendulum has swung in the other direction. "The black comedians and rappers who use and enjoy nigger care principally, perhaps exclusively, about what they themselves think, desire, and enjoy — which is part of their allure. Many people are drawn to these performers despite their many faults because, among other things, they exhibit a bracing independence."

Sadly enough, the "bracing independence" these artists enjoy comes at the expense of their vulnerable fans, who are usually slaves to popular culture. For the sake of the appealing bad boy aura, these artists have subjected millions of fans to a crippling social epidemic that has steadily chipped away at America's traditional values. They have fed into a belief that social (and sometimes legal) boundaries are beyond them. In turn, they have made it evermore difficult for teachers, police, coaches, and parents to co-exist with hip-hop's loyal fans.

5

GOTTA GET THE CASH
GOTTA GET THE DOUGH

"Cash Rules Everything Around Me"
   –   Wu-Tang Clan
"C.R.E.A.M."

Legendary musician B.B. King once revealed in an interview the reason why he sought after a career as a blues performer:

> "I used to get on the street corners and sing when I was about 14 or 15. And I wanted to be a gospel singer. People would come by and ask me to sing a gospel song. When I finished they would always compliment me highly, pat me on my hat or shoulders and say, 'Continue that son. You're going to be great one day.' But they never put nothing in the hat. But people that would ask me to sing the blues would always put something in the hat. So that's why I'm a blues singer."

King makes no bones about the fact that the impetus for his venture into blues wasn't a passion for the music. He makes it quite clear that he could have easily been a gospel singer if the pay were only better.

Incidentally, the paychecks associated with hip-hop are significantly more alluring than the money tossed into King's hat as a young blues performer. As a result, rappers and hip-hop singers plunge haphazardly into a billion-dollar industry that often requires them to exchange their integrity for the unscrupulous practice of exploitation.

Through these exploitative traits, blues and hip-hop artists are able to build lucrative and fruitful careers by selling songs of despair to unwavering fans. For instance, King and others in his genre have simultaneously improved their financial lots and perpetuated commercialized self-sorrow by mass marketing songs like "Bad Luck Soul," "Everyday I Have The Blues," and "How Blue Can You Get."

True to its character, the hip-hop industry has chosen to absorb unadulterated exploitation into its twisted counterculture and present it as an admirable discipline. Nelly perfectly captured the industry's overwhelming sentiments in his song "Ride With Me":

> *If you wanna go and get high with me*
> *Smoke a "L" (marijuana) in the back of the Benzie*
> *Oh, why must I feel this way*
> *Hey, must be the money!*

"The money," to which Nelly credits his inappropriate behavior, is responsible for creating an industry full of hip-hop whores who have shown time and time again they will do anything for a platinum necklace, an expensive car, and a fat bank account. And if the artists are the prostitutes, the industry executives must certainly be recognized as hip-hop's pimps, seeking nothing more than profit margins.

Multi-platinum rap artist Ice Cube, who penned the lyrics to the song "A Bitch is a Bitch," confessed, "As long as I keep selling records that's all they (record executives) care about. Give them a Nazi record, and if they can make money off it, they will."

Unfortunately, the hip-hop industry is replete with artists and wanna-be artists who were reared in financially unstable environments. In their quests to improve their economic status, many of them take on the moral standards of their "pimps" and seek to win fame and fortune by any means necessary.

Trina, hip-hop's self-proclaimed "baddest bitch," is a glaring example. The raunchy rap artist, who grew up in Miami's impoverished Liberty City area, vehemently rejects any notion of returning to her humble beginnings now that she has achieved fame and fortune. "I am not slipping back," she said. "I will do whatever it takes, anything."

Relishing the sweet taste of what hip-hop defines as success, she unashamedly admits the greatest inspiration in her career is money. "I lay in bed with my cash and get off like that," she confessed. "The only thing that motivates me is the cash. Everything else is fucking irrelevant."

It is that Trina-like philosophy of equating self-worth with net worth that has prompted the hip-hop generation to sell its soul for a dollar. Too often, the industry perpetuates the "it's all about the Benjamins" attitude by over-glamorizing the amenities that accompany stardom. The money, the diamond-encrusted platinum jewelry, the $300,000 Bentleys, the designer clothes, and the beautiful groupies flaunted before millions of inspired fans suggest that these are the lone symbols of success and importance. By default, those who have failed to attain these status symbols are less than important and far from successful, according to hip-hop standards.

"What you don't see is what you get"
-     Jay-Z
"Ain't No Nigga"

In the hip-hop spoof *CB-4* starring Chris Rock and Allen Payne, three suburban African American young men struggle to find fame and fortune as a rap trio. Early in the movie they unsuccessfully experiment with different polite rap formats that match their clean-cut image, but it's not until they claim the identity of local thugs that prominent record executive Trustus Jones takes interest. Prior to signing the group to "In Jones We Trust Productions," Jones asked the group five crucial questions:

Jones:	Do you cuss on your records?
CB4:	Yeah!
Jones:	Do you defile women with your lyrics?
CB4:	Uh huh.
Jones:	Do you fondle your genitalia on stage?
CB4:	Whenever possible.
Jones:	Do you glorify violence or advocate the use of guns as a way of solving civil disputes?
CB4:	(Each group member silently pulls out a concealed weapon.)
Jones:	O.K. Final question. Do you guys respect anything at all?
CB4:	Not a damn thing!
Jones:	You got a deal. Welcome to the family!

Although *CB4* may have over-exaggerated the extent to which record executives search for crude acts, many artists recognize the potential gold mines that await them if they cater to the demands of industry executives and prevailing hip-hop trends. The lure of fame and fortune has encouraged many artists to compromise their integrity by assuming degrading public personas that misrepresent their true character.

Writer Clarence Page recognized the growing number of *CB4*-like hip-hop artists and wrote, "It is interesting to note how many of rap's supposedly authentic ghetto voices are in reality offspring of the black middle class dressing down and acting out behavioral stereotypes associated with young low-income blacks, mostly for the consumption of young middle-class whites."

The rap career of Stanley Kirk Burrell, better known as MC Hammer, serves to support Page's claim. As a former church choir director from a middle-class West Coast family, MC Hammer entered the hip-hop industry in the late 1980s as clean-cut, dancing rapper. His energetic dance routines, elaborate live performances, cartoonish costumes, and Disney-friendly party tunes helped establish him as the richest, most prominent rap figure of that time.

In the mid-1990s, however, when the industry began to embrace more risqué acts, MC Hammer's popularity quickly subsided. Instead of succumbing to rap's new era, MC Hammer, who is married with children, reinvented himself, abandoning his Disney audience along the way. No longer would he rap about dancing. The new Hammer, who dropped the "MC" from his moniker and adopted the subtitle "The Funky Headhunter," took a hard left. He replaced his dance garb with a thong in which he danced poolside in a video professing his love for girls "with the pumps and the bumps." His new name, accompanying new thug appearance, and new style of music were quickly dismissed by fans as a pathetic attempt to cling to a fading career.

Hammer's 180-degree makeover ultimately led his career into Billboard obscurity. However, few doubt that his reinvented public persona was prompted by industry trends.

Throughout his career, Hammer, who is now a Christian minister, was recognized within the industry as a "do-gooder."

In fact, he was forced to battle bankruptcy after earning hundreds of millions of dollars because he shared lavishly with his friends, family, and associates. But despite his reputation as one of the good guys, Hammer (like many less scrupulous artists) yielded to the pressure of selling records at any cost.

Unfortunately, it is the unsuspecting fans who endure the dangers of this exploitative practice. They often wholeheartedly buy into the images and messages of these entertainers without knowing the dynamics of such façades.

Aisha Murray Atkins, wife of chart-topping rap artist Ja Rule, admitted that fans sometimes find it difficult to distinguish between the authentic and exploitive messages and images of many artists. Her husband's video "Always on Time" opens with a scene of Ja Rule and several women sprawled out on furniture, asleep after what appears to have been a long night of partying.

"A lot of people think that my husband lives his life the way that he does in his videos," she confessed. But in reality, Ja Rule, a husband and father of two whose birth name is Jeffrey Atkins, doesn't live the life most fans envision. "When I have free time, I'm just sitting at home, doing nothing. I just play with the kids, or I help Britney with her homework."

Like Hammer, many "trend chasers" attempt to build careers in hip-hop based on what's hot at the time. In the 1980s, the industry was replete with acts seeking to capitalize on the "black pride" and "knowledge of self" era. Artists such as X-Clan, Paris, Poor Righteous Teachers, Public Enemy, and KRS-ONE (an acronym for Knowledge Reigns Supreme Over Nearly Everyone) found fame in the hip-hop community by promoting a fusion of education and entertainment called "edutainment."

Today, the tides have changed. Edutainment is no longer the order of the day. Willie D, one-third of the group The Geto Boys, declared, "Preaching that positive bullshit, you can save. Cause your positivity ain't getting' motherfuckers paid."

Willie D's lyrics serve as a warning for aspiring hip-hop artists seeking to land a record deal in an industry that prioritizes gangster imagery. Unfortunately, an artist's admirable intent to enlighten sometimes faces overwhelming odds because the industry's image-makers are transfixed with finding artists who can pad bottom lines. Their capitalist agendas rarely merge with a higher calling of social responsibility, although media giants Tom Joyner and Tavis Smiley have proven the two can coexist.

In lieu of unearthing balanced combinations of capital gains and responsible corporate citizenship, hip-hop executives encourage artists to incorporate the theory of an old farm trick into their exploitative practices. To protect crops from preying animals, many farmers outline their fields with low-voltage electric wire fences. As a cruel and unusual joke, jocular farm workers have been known to grab the arm of an unsuspecting victim with one hand and the electric fence with the other. The stunt sends mild shock waves through the body of the clutched victim, while the prankster in between suffers no pain. As one of science's incongruent laws, the person actually touching the fence is unharmed because his body serves as a conduit that passes electricity to anyone he touches.

In hip-hop, many artists serve as unharmed conduits who pass on electrically-charged lyrics to unsuspecting fans. They often avoid the ramifications of the harmful lyrics they write with one hand and zap the millions of fans they touch with the other. When artists boastfully rap about sexual escapades and brutal acts of violence in the recording studio but quietly retreat to a wife and children after the session, they mislead the fans who seek to replicate their glorified tales of street life.

Ironically, after many of these artists abandon the ghettos that nurture them to greatness and dart for the suburbs, they seem to more vociferously profess their commitment to their roots. Verbally and publicly, they act as if they concur with the sentiments of the rapper Ludacris: "Losing touch with reality is the worse thing that can happen to an entertainer." So to maintain street credibility, hip-hop giants record "tales from the hood" and swear they're "keeping it real."

Conversely, there are some authentic ghetto dwellers who have gained notoriety simply by recounting on record what they have seen and experienced in their neighborhoods. They also claim to be upholding the authenticity of the ghetto, from which hip-hop was derived. But in most of these instances the artists have disguised their visions of multi-platinum paydays with efforts to "keep it real" and ultimately do nothing more than exploit their backgrounds, neighborhoods, and plights.

Never has the act of simply broadcasting ghetto-related stories constituted genuine concern for hip-hop or its constituents. Black Entertainment Television (BET) is the quintessential example. The cable television channel allots only 30 minutes of its 24-hour programming format to a news show dedicated to African American issues.

The company's chairman, Bob Johnson, openly and unashamedly revealed his intentions for the company in talks with social activists who have encouraged him to broaden BET's socially redemptive programming. "The 'E' in BET stands for entertainment, not education," he responded, indicating the station is committed to broadcasting music videos that attract advertising dollars over morally astute programs that enlighten African Americans.

Johnson and BET provide empirical evidence that disseminating ghetto issues doesn't always constitute authentic concern for the ghetto. The station's daily 10 hours of hedonistically-charged videos and raunchy comedy specials do far more damage to the African American community than the good done by its half-hour news show.

The true test of a person's ability to sincerely "keep it real" is his or her commitment to move beyond broadcasting the issues of the ghetto to actually doing something that will improve the blighted conditions they profile. Otherwise they engage in nothing more than lyrical masturbation — a lot of verbal activity that produces nothing.

Hip-hoppers who merely report on ghetto issues exploit the conditions of those communities and leave them no better off than they were before. Therefore, it is illogical, irrational, and certainly irresponsible for artists without activist agendas to parade themselves as ghetto politicians or even strategic partners in the battle to improve the plight of the urban community.

"How much money can one black man make?"
– LL Cool J
"Walking With A Panther"

The creative powers in the hip-hop community, specifically the artists on the Cash Money record label, are responsible for coining the term "bling-bling" to categorize the generation's flamboyant materialistic pursuits. Gaudy jewelry, designer clothes, name-brand sunglasses, flashy cars with oversized tire rims, and even helicopters reign as the symbols of success in this new era of hip-hop. The rapper B.G. managed to capture nearly all of these aspirations in one verse:

I be that nigga with the ice (diamonds) on me
If it cost less than twenty ($20,000) it don't look right on me

I stay flossed out (flamboyant) all through the week
My money long, if you don't know I'm the B.G.
I be fuckin' niggaz' bitches all in they home
Niggaz be like, "Look at that Benz on all that chrome"
Diamonds worn by everybody that's in my clique
Man, I got the price of a mansion 'round my neck and wrist
My nigga Baby gettin' a special-built machine
A Mercedes Benz 700 V14
I know you niggaz can't believe that
I can't wait to see ya haters' face when ya see that
Man, look at that
Niggaz wear shades just to stand on side of me
Folks say, "Take that chain off, boy, ya blindin' me"
All day my phone ringin'
Bling bling bling
You can see my earring from a mile
Bling bling

Scores of critics are bent on condemning the ostentatious aspirations of B.G. and others from the hip-hop generation, claiming their flashy pursuits cause fans to dangerously equate net worth with self-worth. Their fear is that hip-hop's materialistic agenda will sidetrack fans from more substantive issues.

Factually, there assessments couldn't be more correct. Instead of tackling social issues like racial profiling, AIDS, or the digital divide, many of the most brilliant hip-hop minds have yet to discover their full potential because they're obsessed with thoughts of platinum jewelry and Bentleys.

But what the critics don't mention is that many of *them* were grooving to lyrics like "diamond in the back, sunroof top, digging the scene with a gangsta lean" more than a decade before hip-hop blossomed. They lambaste hip-hop without scrutinizing the "bling-bling" demonstrations of *their* adolescent years, which easily could have served as benchmarks for contemporary models of materialism.

Therefore, the legitimate concern isn't necessarily that hip-hop has a penchant for gaudy goods. After all, those traits can be found in every generation. The more notable concern is that when it comes to materialistic pursuits and anything else, hip-hop has a propensity to overindulge. Like eating pork, the culture's materialistic pursuits would be far less harmful if practiced moderately. Unfortunately, its excessive diet of "bling-bling" creates an unhealthy community that improperly prioritizes cars over careers, diamonds over degrees, and Courvoisier over communion.

There is nothing inherently wrong with hip-hoppers wanting or having nice things. But the culture's unprecedented levels of overt covetousness have set off societal alarms that should serve as wake-up calls for those interested in reclaiming a misguided generation.

6

FREAKY TALES

"I remember how it all began.
I used to sing dirty raps to my eastside fans."
— Too Short
"Life Is Too Short"

Once while on a business trip in Chicago, I ate dinner in a mall food court next to a group of black and white middle school girls. Their giggling, gossiping, and chattering came to a halt when a handsome young boy walked by their table. They all gazed at him as he searched for a place to eat in the busy food court. Instantly, as he took his seat across the room, the silence at the young girls' table was broken by several deep sighs and screams of adoration.

Their conversation quickly pivoted to discussions about the boy and how each of them might win his heart. After pondering several strategies, the girls finally concluded that the best way to lure the young man was to appeal to his sensual urges. "I know what we should do," one girl recommended. "Go past his table with our 'Marilyn Monroe' walks. That'll get his attention."

Despite being articulate, personable, and seemingly well educated, these young girls were prepared to surrender all their positive attributes and rely on sex appeal to make an impression.

Like those young girls, the hip-hop industry has its own crop of red-light-district artists who have surrendered their authentic artistic traits and settled for the less-demanding challenge of selling sex.

I left the food court before the girls paraded themselves in front of that unsuspecting young boy, therefore, I can't conclude with any certainty if they were successful in luring him into their adolescent web of temptation. But with more than fifteen years of accruing sexual content, there's no denying the success hip-hop has had in baiting its hormone-driven fans.

———

Hip-hop's first notable forays into crude mass-marketed sexuality can be traced to Too Short and 2 Live Crew. The songs "Freaky Tales" and "Don't Fight the Feelin'," released in the mid- to late-1980s, helped launch the still-thriving career of Too Short. Since then, Too Short has released more than 10 albums that have not strayed from his original formula, most of which have gone gold or platinum.

2 Live Crew's breakout album in 1989 left few doubts about the group's interest in redemptive entertainment. The controversy behind the album *As Nasty As They Wanna Be*—which was chock-full of X-rated songs like "Me So Horny," "Dick Almighty," and "The Fuck Shop"—helped propel the group into another stratosphere of notoriety and listed them among the industry's pioneers.

Though it would be several more years before similar smut-laden songs and artists saturated the market, the early strategies of Too Short and 2 Live Crew can be significantly credited for designing hip-hop's X-rated blueprints.

With these models in place to help them navigate hip-hop's new terrain, a groundswell of new uncouth rappers and hip-hop singers made attempts to cash in on a generation of fans who were coming to terms with their sexuality.

Groups like Bytches Wit Problems and Hoes With Attitude made lackluster attempts to introduce women into what was then a male-dominated genre. But females interested in entering hip-hop's sensual spotlight would have to wait until Tone Loc's "Wild Thing," Sir Mix-A-Lot's "Baby Got Back," and H-Town's "Knockin' the Boots" helped softened the market.

Today, the market is ripe with both male and female artists who, like R. Kelly, "don't see nothin' wrong with a little bump and grind." The *LyricScan* study of 2001's top hip-hop songs helped quantify the pervasiveness of this new sexual era.

Among the six tunes nominated for single of the year were 73 sexual references: 1 educational, 42 subtle, and 30 lewd.

These statistics, unfortunately, represent a new era in which Missy Elliott encourages fans to "Get Your Freak On" but not with a "One Minute Man." Bubba Sparxxx warns women they "won't see tomorrow if I don't cut (have sex) tonight." Tyrese and Da Brat ask, "What do you like? A whole lot of foreplay right before you get it started?"

"Oops! There goes my skirt, dropping to my feet," is Tweet's contribution. Lil' Kim confesses, "I used to be scared of the dick. Now I throw lips to the shit. Handle it like a real bitch." Foxy Brown tells men, "Taste my na-na in the rain on the hood of your car or the back of the plane." And in her chart-topping song "My Neck, My Back," the "Thug Misses" Khia instructs, "Lick it now. Lick it good. Lick this pussy just like you should."

To further its cause, this hip-hop sexual revolution has managed to transcend mere lyrical displays. Today, most hip-hop songs are accompanied by sexually charged music videos that are packaged with the standard shapely, scantily clad, oiled-down women profiled in provocative positions.

This trend has become so pervasive that BET has dedicated a one-hour, late-night time slot to air the most controversial of these borderline pornographic music videos. It's not uncommon to turn to any of BET's 3 a.m. segments of *Un:Cut* and witness a full hour of strippers dancing in thong swimsuits while rappers make uncouth artistic attempts to fondle them and perform at the same time.

The boundaries of this hip-hop sexual revolution have stretched even further to include the industry's print media. *The Source* and *XXL* have contributed to the uprising of hard-core hip-hop sexuality by going beyond the practice of merely reporting the trends of the industry.

In February 2002, *The Source* disseminated its "Sex Issue," which featured candid surveys and articles about closet freaks, sexual positions, threesomes, anal sex, foot fetishes, adultery, and oral sex. In addition, the issue featured a six-page fashion spread of provocatively dressed women. The introductory tagline for the spread read: "Nothing makes you sweat like hot spring wears. Peek into the girls' locker room, where the gear is sporty and the girls are sweet as candy."

To add fuel to the sexual fire, *The Source* features an annual swimsuit edition while *XXL* has a monthly "eye candy" profile. Neither serves much of a purpose other than to entice readers who have grown accustomed to having a little sex with their hip-hop.

And to legitimize hip-hop's venture into the sex arena, rappers like Snoop Dogg, Humpty Hump, Money B, and Treach have officially crossed the line into the world of adult pornography. In 2002, Snoop's *Hustler*-distributed *Doggystyle* porn video received best music and top-selling tape honors at the Adult Video Awards. The film, which was recorded at

Snoop's house, featured the rapper performing his songs while several porno stars had sex around him.

Naughty By Nature member and actor Treach raised a few eyebrows when he decided to take part in a porno movie. "Initially it was something that we did for the women who may have fantasies or aspirations about being with me or that type of thing. There's a market out there for this type of thing," Treach said.

———————

Despite hip-hop's mounting X-rated campaign, a 2002 national survey on *Teens, Sex and TV* found a bittersweet silver lining in the sexual content on television shows and music videos. The survey, conducted by *US News & World Report* and the Kaiser Family Foundation, revealed that many teens feel they have learned how to say no to a sexual situation that makes them uncomfortable (60 percent) and how to talk to a partner about safer sex (43 percent) because of sexual scenes on television.

However, conflicting statistics in that same survey highlight an unfortunate dilemma among today's youth that corroborate theories on influence supported by many hip-hop critics. Nearly three out of four fifteen- to seventeen-year-olds (72 percent) reported that sexual content on television influences the behavior of teenagers their age. In other words, they believe that young girls are persuaded to pattern their sexuality after the half-dressed sex objects who parade themselves around like prostitutes in hip-hop music videos. Likewise, these teenagers suspect that young boys will adopt the spontaneous, non-committal sex patterns portrayed by the men in hip-hop videos—men who only seem to have interest in the aforementioned women.

Those who are inclined to dismiss the beliefs of the youth in this survey will likely counter with a valid question: Does watching hip-hop videos *really* make kids want to have sex? The correct answer is no. Music videos don't make kids want to have sex. God does! *He* wired us (especially teenagers) to instinctively crave sex. That's simply part of our human nature.

However, raunchy hip-hop videos can take significant credit for exacerbating the growing amount of irresponsible, promiscuous sexual behavior among influential fans. The industry's relentless barrage of seductive videos and lyrical foreplay add reckless fuel to the hormonal fires brewing in many of these teenagers.

Responding to the question of "Is hip-hop oversexed," Ludacris answered, "Hell nah." The rapper explained, "People will never get tired of talking about sex or seeing it. That's why you've got, like, HBO's *Real Sex* 115 and shit. One of our biggest emotions is love and probably the next one is lust. Sex sells-- plain and simple."

Ludacris is wrong in his answer but right in his assessment. Hip-hop is oversexed! Whenever Lil' Kim celebrates her sexual prowess by proclaiming her ability to make a Sprite can disappear in her mouth on an adolescent-oriented music video show (BET's *106 & Park*), there's not much debating the fact that hip-hop has invested too much stock in sex.

Sex sells because it is one of the most intense and innate of all the human traits. It is one of the most recognizable commonalities among races, genders, classes, nationalities, and age groups. And proof of its fondness can be found in the world's ever-growing population.

Because this animal-like instinct has such mass appeal, it only stands to reason that hip-hoppers (along with artists and executives in every other entertainment genre) would make efforts to cash in on it. They make songs, videos, movies, and magazine spreads that cater to this basic instinct. What's more, they have the audacity to honor many of these bottom-feeding capitalistic ploys as the best products the genre has to offer.

Consider how much talent it would take for a person to sell a plain cracker to a man who hadn't eaten in five days. Most people intelligent enough to read this book would agree that that would be a simple, non-challenging transaction for any salesperson. That's because it doesn't take much talent to sell crackers to a man desperately trying to fulfill his most basic need for food.

True talent can be assessed in a person's ability to sell a plain cracker to a man who has just finished eating Thanksgiving dinner. His appetite would be so thoroughly satiated that he wouldn't find gratification in something as simple as crackers.

But for some baffling reason, the entertainment industry relishes the idea of selling proverbial sex crackers to its fans. Many artists make a habit of marketing to fans' lowest instinctual thresholds and then receive awards for selling sex to sex-craved patrons.

The 2001 MTV Video Awards provides a quintessential example. Instead of honoring any one of the many conceptually unique music videos made that year, MTV selected "Lady Marmalade" for the Video of the Year award. The song, a remake of the 1974 hit by Labelle, introduced the hip-hop community to the dated French phrase "Voulez-vous coucher avec moi, ce soir." (Translation: "Do you want to sleep with me tonight?")

As to be expected, the concept for the "Lady Marmalade" video, which featured Lil' Kim, Pink, Mya, Missy Elliott, and Christina Aguilera, revolved around the song's sexual inquiry. In the video, the young ladies performed their respective verses in a whorehouse while they prepared for a night's work. And seemingly for nothing more than wearing lingerie and portraying themselves as prostitutes, the

"Marmalade" ladies were honored with MTV's most prestigious award.

"I nearly died when I saw she was wearing so little," commented Delcie Fidler after seeing her granddaughter Christina Aguilera in the video. "What gets me is that Christina thinks she is doing something clever, but anyone can strip," she added.

Unfortunately, Christina and others in the entertainment industry have failed to heed Grandma's wisdom. Instead, they have lowered the standards of the industry by selling plain crackers to a fan base that is feasting on an unhealthy smorgasbord of sex.

7

PRAYER HATERS

"What good will it be for a man
if he gains the world, yet forfeits his soul?"
    – Jesus Christ
    Matthew 16:26

It's nearly impossible to attend a concert, read hip-hop magazines, or watch music videos without noticing the holy crosses that adorn the necklaces worn by many hip-hop figures. These religious symbols represent the method by which human salvation was rendered when Jesus Christ was crucified on a wooden cross over 2,000 years ago for the sins of all mankind.

Those who fashionably sport the cross are generally thought to be making a public declaration of their belief in the Christian faith. Their expensive, diamond-encrusted crosses say more than "look at me!" They say, "Look at me. I'm a Christian!"

Some artists, including Ludacris, have chosen to go beyond the optional act of adorning jewelry to make an outward profession of faith. Instead, they opt for more permanent religious identification with tattoos of praying hands, crosses, and other spiritual symbols.

And as if these gestures aren't enough to convince others of their belief in a higher power (be it Jesus, Allah, or Buddha), many performers lightly sprinkle their musical compilations with distinct references to God or the afterlife. Albums and songs like "God's Son" (Nas), "I Wonder If Heaven Got A Ghetto," (Tupac), and "Forgive Them Father" (Lauryn Hill) ring familiar in many hip-hop circles.

But despite all the public professions of faith made within the hip-hop community, a conspicuous contradiction of holy beliefs and unholy protocols permeate the industry.

Missy Elliott, applauded for her hit song "Get Your Freak On," epitomized this holy irony in her acceptance speech for the best R&B, Soul, or Rap music video at the 2002 Soul Train Awards. "First of all, I wanna give honor to God," she said. "I'm real religious. I know I sing a lot of crazy music, but I'm real religious. And I know this is God right here that got me right here."

The dichotomy found in hip-hop artists like Elliott who promote sexual immorality, violence, greed, and contemptuous behavior yet have the audacity to give thanks to a God that condemns those traits is baffling. Their oxymoronic praise is about as sensible as a married man thanking God for an adulterous relationship. Surely, the teachings of Jesus and

Muhammad, the leaders of the two most prominent religions in hip-hop, don't condone such behavior.

An exploration of the Holy Scriptures exposes the many blatant contradictions that exist between hip-hop and popular religion.

ISSUE	HOLY BIBLE	HIP-HOP
Sexual Immorality	"It is God's will that you should be sanctified: that you should avoid sexual immorality" -- 1 Thessalonians 4:3	"No panties coming off. My love is gonna cost. Cause ain't no way that you gonna get up in this for free" -- Trina, "No Panties"
Adultery	"You shall not commit adultery." -- Deuteronomy 5:18	"I already got a wife. Can't leave you alone. And I know I'm living wrong. But I can't let you go" -- Fabolous, "Can't Let You Go"
Drunkards	"Do not get drunk on wine, which leads to debauchery." -- Ephesians 5:18	"Drink Yack (cognac) 'til I'm falling out" -- P. Diddy, "Pass the Courvoisier"
Greed	"Watch out! Be on your guard against all kinds of greed; a man's life does not consist in the abundance of his possessions." -- Luke 12:15	"Slide me 200 G's ($200,000) and I'll do anything" -- Big Tymers "Put That Shit Up"
Murder	"You shall not commit murder." -- Deuteronomy 5:17	"Sun in to sun out, I'ma keep the gun out. Nigga runnin his mouth? I'ma blow his lung out." -- DMX, "Party Up"
Contempt	"Do not use harmful words, but only helpful words, the kind that build up and provide what is needed, so that what you say will do good to those who hear you." -- Ephesians 4:29	"Move bitch! Get out the way!" -- Ludacris "Move Bitch"
Evil	"Turn from evil and do good; seek peace and pursue it." -- Psalms 34:14	"All I wanted to do was rape the bitch and snatch her purse. Now I wanna kill her." -- Eminem, "As the World Turns"

It doesn't take a theologian to recognize that hip-hop and the Holy Scriptures are not on parallel tracks. It appears that when religion says go right, hip-hop artists not only go left, but make a mockery of the sacred by thanking God for blessing their vile actions.

What's worse is many hip-hop artists clutter this juxtaposition by misinterpreting the scriptures in their favor to justify the wrong they do. For instance, in defense of their behavior, they encourage others not to judge them because the "Bible says so."

A thorough search of the scriptures reveals this as a partial truth. Matthew 7 begins by warning Christians, "Do not judge." That's usually as far as most scrutinized hip-hop artists read. In its entirety, the warning reads, "Do no judge, or you too will be judged. For in the same way you judge others, you will be judged and with the measure you use, it will be measured to you."

The inference in this message is not to avoid judging. Instead, it is a warning that critics will be judged by the same standards they judge others.

In the best-case scenario, this scripture warning would inspire would-be critics to live up to a high level of integrity before attempting to criticize others. In the worst-case scenario, no one would have the gumption to criticize anyone else because of rampant low moral standards. Biblically, however, critics who promote sexual immorality, adultery, murder, or greed in other formats will be subjected to the same level of criticism they hold for hip-hop's heathens.

Another favorite scripture justification for hip-hop's wayward Christians is Romans 3:23: "For all have sinned and fallen short of the glory of God." Errant hip-hoppers like to use this scripture to remind critics that no one is exempt from sin, which suggests that when they "fall short" they're simply fulfilling a Biblical prophecy.

However, these hip-hop defendants conveniently overlook the many scriptures that warn of the ultimate demise of those who partake in persistent, premeditated sin. Hebrews 10:26-27 warns, "If we deliberately keep on sinning after we have received the knowledge of the truth, no sacrifice for sins is left, but only a fearful expectation of judgment and of raging fire that will consume the enemies of God."

For artists with a healthy fear of God, this scripture should serve as a wake-up call because it clearly condemns the premeditated sin to which many of them readily yield. Within the Christian faith, an occasional sin is expected, but it doesn't accommodate those who know of God's commandments yet deliberately disobey them.

That's bad news for artists who know that sexual immorality, greed, contemptuousness, and drunkenness are condemned by God yet spend years writing, producing, and marketing songs that promote these blasphemous traits. The

Bible says these artists can expect "judgment" and "raging fire" in return for their acts of calculated transgression.

But Christians aren't the only hip-hop artists guilty of religious apostasy. Emerging rapper Freeway was reared as a devout Muslim yet now wallows in hip-hop's sacrilegious cesspool. Despite being cognizant of the Islamic principle that requires its believers to think five times before doing anything, Freeway launched his rap career with lyrics that tout murder and his life as a drug dealer.

Freeway and other Muslim rappers stand in clear violation of the Islamic faith and the teachings of Nation of Islam leader Minister Louis Farrakhan. Farrakhan encouraged rappers at the 2002 West Coast Hip-Hop Summit to "take up the mantle of leadership and pray to God to help you use your talents." The minister, who served as keynote speaker at the summit, further encouraged rappers to "become architects of a brand-new world. Rise to your divinity and help us get back to our humanity."

———————

The destiny of wayward hip-hop artists becomes even more frightening when Jesus' warning to spare the children is taken into consideration. In Matthew 18:6 he said, "But if anyone causes one of these little ones who believes in me to sin, it would be better for him to have a large millstone hung around his neck and to be drowned in the depths of the sea."

As this book has revealed, children are heavily influenced by the sacrilegious messages and images portrayed within the hip-hop community. As such, Jesus' warning doesn't bode well for the artists who inspire young fans to disobey the teachings of the Bible.

A notable example of such a violation is Jay-Z's breach of the third commandment, which advises in Deuteronomy 5:11, "Do not use my name for evil purposes for I, the Lord your God, will punish anyone who misuses my name."

But despite the scripture's advisory, Jay-Z wrote and heavily marketed his 2001 hit song "H.O.V.A." to a nation of children who happily and blindly sang along as he referenced *himself* as Jay-H.O.V.A. And to ensure there was no misunderstanding about Jay-Z's implication for the song, the online publicist for his record label's Web site confirmed that *H.O.V.A.* is a play on Jehovah, ancient Israel's sacred word for God.

Jay-Z's religious contravention is not easily overlooked—even by the people who have cashed in on his success. Russell Simmons, whose record label helps market and distribute Jay-Z's music, noted that Jay-Z would take you "right to hell" with the power he wields over young fans.

"If from age one to adulthood all you heard was Jay-Z, you're gonna learn to get ahead of everybody and fight the world," he said. "You're gonna learn to kill. You know what? A baby will go right to hell fuckin' with Jay-Z, but that baby will be wearing the hottest designer shit and driving the hottest car with the coolest rims."

Simmons' bold observation easily doubles as a confession that every dollar used to produce, market, and promote Jay-Z's music — which equates to millions — is a dollar used to help send his young fans to hell.

———

For John Walker Lindh, Jay-Z may not have been the culprit that helped prepare his path to hell on earth, but the decadent traits of hip-hop can not be excused from the role they played in helping to establish him as one of America's most famous traitors in recent history. Walker Lindh, a white Northern Californian "seeker," abandoned the soil and freedom of America to unite with Afghanistan's Taliban army after an unfulfilled soul-searching trek led him through the dismal boroughs of hip-hop.

At the age of 14, years before Walker Lindh's affiliation with Osama bin Laden's terrorist group, he began frequenting several crude hip-hop Web sites and daringly left a message on one that read, "Our blackness should not make white people hate us."

After several more years in the world of hip-hop, Walker disavowed the music and the culture partly because of its religious hypocrisies. He took particular issue with the rapper

Nas, who is referred to as a god in certain hip-hop circles. "If this is so," Walker Lindh said indignantly of Nas, "then why does he smoke blunts, drink Moet, fornicate, and make dukey music? That's a rather pathetic god, if you ask me." Reports indicate that Walker Lindh soon afterwards sold off his rap CD collection, converted to Islam, and joined an army that would eventually orchestrate the most heinous terrorist attack on American soil.

Few would deny that Walker Lindh's tumultuous tango with hip-hop came at a vulnerable time in his life when he found himself wrestling with a slippery identity and attempting to grasp the answers to many of life's thorny questions. During that time, he was unfortunately greeted with hip-hop's theology of marketed hate, greed, nihilism, overindulgence, and irreverence for God. Consequently, he dissociated himself with the culture and sought refuge in Islam's most notorious sect. What an insult to hip-hop!

Walker Lindh's defection to Afghanistan proved that hip-hop couldn't deliver the goods when it really mattered. After all, what better time is there to welcome someone into the hip-hop culture than when they're earnestly seeking acceptance? But unlike the many content fans who pledge allegiance to hip-hop, Walker was searching for something more than the culture could provide. He wanted substance. He wanted purpose. He wanted discipline. He wanted truth. And hip-hop didn't have much of it to give.

Walker Lindh was sentenced to 20 years in a federal prison after a plea agreement that found him guilty of providing services to the Taliban while armed. Other than maybe his parents, few would disagree that it is the responsibility of the United States to hold Walker accountable for the role he played in the September 11, 2001, sabotage of the lives and safety of thousands of innocent American families.

But surprisingly, there seem to be few concerned with taking hip-hop to task for its al-Qaeda-like practices that have done more to threaten the safety, intellectual capacities, health, freedom, and futures of its American constituents than John Walker Lindh ever has.

It could be al-Qaeda's cult fixation with murder that has America preoccupied with thwarting foreign terrorists and not hip-hop. If so, America doesn't have to look any further than Ja Rule, who records music for the Murder Inc. imprint, to know that there's a battle to be fought on the home soil.

After winning the Single of the Year award at the 2001 Source Awards, Ja Rule began his acceptance speech by emphatically proclaiming, "The Murder Inc. has arrived!" He punctuated his proclamation by saying, "Yo, first off I want to thank God." His contrasting statements don't lend themselves to Christianity, Islam, or any other respectable religion. Only al-Qaeda-like sects, which took pride in demolishing the World Trade Centers, would find it honorable to associate their god with murder. But, surprisingly, no one batted an eye when one of hip-hop's most prominent icons aligned his god with what he considers fashionable homicide.

And in a continued state of blasphemy Ja Rule suggested to reporters that a potential collaboration between him and Nas be called the "gods' albums cause me and Nas both have biblical names." He went on to say of Nas' rumored plan to join the Murder Inc. family that, "It's a thing that might really get crazy." Crazy indeed, Ja Rule. Crazy indeed.

But it may not be al-Qaeda's terrorist agenda that has caused America to postpone chastising hip-hop. It could be Walker Lindh's open affiliation with the cult that allows the country to take comfort in prioritizing his judgment and conviction over that of the wayward culture. If so, it would appear that many Americans have failed to realize they have been sleeping with the terrorist enemy of hip-hop for years.

The biblical assessment of hip-hop-like cultures offers an accurate picture:

> "They have become filled with every kind of wickedness, evil, greed, and depravity. They are full of envy, murder, strife, deceit, and malice. They are gossips, slanderers, God-haters, insolent, arrogant and boastful; they invent ways of doing evil; they disobey their parents; they are senseless, faithless, heartless, ruthless. Although they know God's righteous decree that those who do such things deserve death, they not only continue to do these very things but also approve of those who practice them." – *Romans 2:29-32*

8

WHERE DO WE GO FROM HERE?

"Every man must decide whether he will walk in the light of creative altruism or the darkness of destructive selfishness."
— Martin Luther King, Jr.

For those of us who drive, cruising down boulevards and passing through busy intersections isn't usually considered risky. Many people do it every day with no consequence. But remove the stop signs that govern our driving, and those routine tasks suddenly become high-stakes gambling scenarios. That's because an imminent danger lurks in a society's inability to discern when to stop, go, or yield.

In a very real example, a group of adolescent boys removed all of the stop signs from their neighborhood as a thoughtless prank. Consequently, the drivers who navigated the streets in that community assumed they were free to drive without yielding to anyone or anything.

What ensued was a rash of tragic automobile accidents that threatened the lives of many unsuspecting people. This juvenile practical joke that was intended to produce a few laughs instead caused chaos by devaluing the governing laws of the road.

It is that same principle of ungoverned traffic that has produced hip-hop's chaotic landscape. In a very similar manner, those associated with the culture have uprooted many of hip-hop's intangible stop signs and subsequently harmed many of those who navigate its terrain.

Clearly, the stop sign that precedes the road of disrespect has been removed from hip-hop's structural grid and has produced a generation that finds delight in the lyrics "Move, bitch! Get out the way!"

Hip-hop's reckless abandon for sex suggests that the stop sign at the road of sexual immorality has been discarded as well.

And the ability of parents, the government, and the media to often ignore the negative impact hip-hop has on its impressionable fans suggests that a yield marker has replaced the stop sign that once sat atop the road of passionate activism.

Therefore, it only stands to reason that the best strategy to restore decency and order to hip-hop is to reinstall the many uprooted stop signs that made the culture great once upon a time.

This doesn't suggest that hip-hop's restoration strategy include journeys back to the good ol' days when the culture thrived under a different set of standards. Many nostalgic fans would love nothing more than to rewind hip-hop back 15 years to the time when Young MC loved to "Bust a Move" and MC Hammer was "Too Legit to Quit." Their rationale, which does bear some legitimacy, suggests that any former era of hip-hop would be more appropriate than the one to which they're held captive today.

However, some things are best left in the past— especially Young MC's elementary lyrics and those wack Hammer pants. But solace for nostalgic fans might be found in the poignant rebuttal of C.S. Lewis regarding the notion of celebrating the standards of yesteryear:

> "I would rather get away from the whole idea of clocks. We all want progress. But progress means getting nearer to the place where you want to be. And if you have taken a wrong turning, then to go forward does not get you any nearer. If you are on the wrong road, progress means doing an about-turn and walking back to the right road; and in that case the man who turns back soonest is the most progressive . . . . [and] going back is the quickest way on."

A practical application of Lewis' philosophy is to marry the lyrical proficiency of today's best hip-hop artists and the superb musical creations of its best producers to the heightened standards of consciousness and responsibility from yesteryear. The intent is to create a functional evolution strategy for the culture instead of allowing it to dissolve in its inability to walk back to the right road.

But undoubtedly, arranging a merger of hip-hop's greatest skill sets, its greatest measures of responsibility, and its greatest potentials is a multifaceted task that requires multifaceted solutions. The participants in such a noble endeavor must be nothing short of radical revolutionaries. They must be brave. They must be passionate. They must be longsuffering. They must prioritize people over profits. And they must be unwavering.

The sad reality is that not enough people with the aforementioned traits have answered the call to restore hip-hop. But this absence of leadership isn't confirmation that society at large has accepted the standards of the wayward culture. They haven't! They just haven't accepted the call to action.

In the heat of the Civil Rights movement, Dr. King assessed America's racist agenda and concluded that the greatest impediment preventing African Americans from obtaining equality wasn't the Ku Klux Klan. It wasn't the good-old-boy networks. And it wasn't racist politicians. King determined that the quest for racial equality was most threatened by the many millions of privileged white people who empathized with the civil rights struggle yet never lent their support to the cause. Because of their inactivity, a larger burden of responsibility was placed on a disproportionately smaller group of activists to convince America that institutionalized racism is unhealthy.

Likewise, in the quest to improve hip-hop, the greatest obstacles aren't Jay-Z, Lil' Kim, Trina, Eminem, Ludacris, or The

Hot Boyz. The single greatest challenge facing hip-hop restoration activists is the task of motivating empathetic critics to assume active roles in the struggle.

Every time a parent's frustration with hip-hop is met with inactivity, the hope of restoring the culture takes a step backward. Every time a music executive ignores the dysfunctional traits of an artist, the decadent patterns of hip-hop are expedited. And every time a consumer buys an album with lyrics that contradict his personal beliefs, the Hip-Hop Holocaust gains financial footing to spew its messages far and wide.

To save what's left of the culture and possibly redirect it, the legions of inactive hip-hop critics must share in the efforts of those who are committed to promoting, producing, and protecting the best of hip-hop. Thus the last and most important chapter of this book focuses on strategies to empower those idle empathizers in a way that will ultimately rehabilitate the culture and those who have contributed to its moral decay.

Parents Just Don't Understand

No group of proponents has a more legitimate opportunity to turn the tides of the hip-hop culture than parents. In fact, because of the power they wield, parents have the greatest responsibility to ensure hip-hop's largest fan base doesn't succumb to the perils of the culture.

Abdicating that responsibility, as too many parents often do, should not be an option. But because it is, a long list of consequences and repercussions trouble our society.

If parents are to accept this challenge of swinging the hip-hop pendulum, they must abandon the lame parenting techniques that have made an inordinate amount of room for substandard values and behavior. That doesn't necessarily mean that all parents must follow the example of Tipper Gore and create organizations to battle the ills of the music industry. After all, not everyone is equipped with the resources and know-how to take on a billion-dollar Goliath.

But a common strategy that every parent can employ is to ditch the adage "Do as I say, not as I do." That parenting technique is no longer the effective disciplinary tool it once was years ago. Children want and desperately need examples of how they should behave.

That means when they see their parents affirm crass hip-hop music by listening to it themselves, they as model-seeking children are less likely to develop a conscience that raises red flags when their favorite artist crosses the line of decency. Furthermore, it ruins any credible chance parents have of teaching children what's right and wrong with hip-hop.

During the summer of 2002, Nelly's song "Hot in Herre" became the most played tune on radio and music video programs with 6,933 spins. It would behoove parents to know that was nearly 7,000 times their children were prompted by the rapper to "take off all your clothes."

To not know that such lyrics are inundating the minds of children is a parenting travesty. But conversely, it is a daunting full-time task for any parent seeking to single-handedly learn the lyrical content of all the music their children take interest in.

Thus the legitimacy of the parenting aids *LyricScan* and V-Chip. These two revolutionary tools were created to assist parents in the task of filtering inappropriate entertainment from their children's media diets.

LyricScan, referenced in Chapter 2, is a free service that publishes the lyrical ingredients of popular songs after sifting them for uses of profanity, racial epithets, and references to sex, drugs, alcohol, violence, and contemptuous behavior. (The service can be accessed at: www.AAOReport.com.)

The V-Chip is a device required in most televisions that enables parents to block programs (including music video shows) they consider inappropriate for their children.

These supplemental parenting tools can be great assets to parents who are serious about providing safeguards for their children. In addition, they provide the grassroots strategies necessary to gain the attention of the hip-hop powers-that-be.

The Incorrigible Fan

Headlines rarely speak well of hip-hop fans. They usually tell of their notorious propensities for violent acts, drug use, and sexual indiscretions. For instance, news wires were set ablaze with separate stories of two fans who were presumably prompted to commit murder after listening to aggressive songs by Tupac and Ludacris.

Editors got a good laugh from the story that told of a judge's unique sentence of a seventeen-year-old who was arrested for possession of drug paraphernalia. Judge Nancy Dusek-Gomez sentenced Matthew Fournier to listen to and write a report on Afroman's song "I Got High" while paying particular attention to the line "Now, I'm a quadriplegic and know why, because I got high."

Combine these stories with the many that tell of the violence (or fear of violence) at hip-hop venues, and an obvious slant in media coverage begins to rear its head. That slant is often commensurate with the unbalanced, negative listening habits of the fans who make the headlines.

Just as balanced diets are necessary to maintain healthy bodies, balanced listening habits are essential in producing well-rounded hip-hop fans. What people feed their minds is just as important as what they feed their bodies. Unfortunately, in the same way that Americans have rendered themselves unhealthy by succumbing to junk-food diets, too many fans have tainted their minds by feasting on diets of crude, immoral hip-hop.

For traditional diets, nutritionists recommended that meals be balanced with breads and cereals; fruits and vegetables; meat and dairy products; and sparing helpings of fats, sweets, and oils. Fats, sweets, and oils are considered junk foods that have proven to be unhealthy when taken in large doses.

For healthy entertainment diets, it is important that fans receive balanced portions of romantic and intellectual stimuli, the blues and comic relief, social issues and festive offerings, and spiritual and secular renderings. Regrettably, the coexistence of these offerings has become increasingly rare in hip-hop. Instead, fans gorge on hip-hop slop made of freaky tales, thug lullabies, and bling-bling aspirations, which reveals their unwillingness to adhere to the rule of moderation necessary in maintaining a healthy entertainment diet.

They don't realize that hip-hop slop is like pork—if you consume it in moderation it won't hurt you. But if you digest too much, it can kill you.

Therefore, it would behoove hip-hop fans to ensure their entertainment diets are balanced with the appropriate mix of hip-hop nutrients. Likewise, they should challenge their favorite artists to offer entertainment that supports their needs. By doing so, they might change the headlines that reflect so poorly on them.

The Leadership Blind Spot

As if the challenges of refashioning hip-hop were not great enough, the dichotomy posed by those in prominent leadership positions convolute the matter even more. On one hand, leaders like Minister Louis Farrakhan know that rappers are "second moms and dads to those who listen to" them and therefore challenge them to create "more educational raps and more rappers willing to teach since so many kids won't go to school." On the other hand, the pastor of one of Atlanta's largest Christian congregations makes himself available for a cameo appearance in the music video "Welcome To Atlanta," which is laced with lyrics about strip joints, gangsters, and all-night parties where attendees can get "fucked up."

For the sake of connecting with hip-hop's largely self-indulgent generation, too many of our nation's leaders have compromised their ability to render effective critiques of the hip-hop culture. The lure of establishing a hip-hop constituency has caused many of them to seek credibility with this lost generation by finding footing on many of the culture's decadent platforms. Instead of courageously calling a spade a spade, they too often result to the cowardly tactic of ignoring, downplaying, or applauding hip-hop's pitfalls and the people who create them.

During the 2001 Source Awards, Jesse Jackson added himself to this growing list of compromised leaders. Prior to presenting LL Cool J with a Lifetime Achievement Award, the renowned civil rights leader greeted the audience with a sly smile and the popular hip-hop pig Latin phrase, "Fo shizzle, my nizzle," which means, "For sure, my nigga."

Although there is great wisdom in the disciplinary theory "you must connect before you correct," Jackson significantly lessened his chances of influencing wayward hip-hop artists when he crossed an obvious line of decency himself. His inappropriate behavior at the Source Awards did more to condone and encourage the rampant immoral traits in hip-hop than to correct those who have pledged allegiance to thug life.

But Jackson doesn't stand alone on the side of failed leadership in this unfortunate dichotomy. He's accompanied by many other leaders who have attempted to cozy up to hip-hop in ways that forsake their responsibility to promote and protect the moral high-road.

This growing leadership divide was profoundly pronounced in Missouri where politicians wrangled over Governor Bob Holden's decision to honor popular St. Louis rapper Nelly for his pledge to support high schools that increase their participation in standardized testing. Citing his lyrics as inappropriate and detrimental to the proper development of young fans, some Missouri politicians protested the award ceremony held in Nelly's honor.

Had it been from an ordinary Joe off the street, a pledge of support to the school system would not have meant as much to Holden. The protesting politicians understood that it was Nelly's fame that made his support significant to the governor. That, in and of itself, was not a problem. But what was of significant concern to them was the *route* Nelly took to fame and fortune.

He skyrocketed to international prominence by writing and performing youth-oriented songs replete with salacious lyrics. That, in the eyes of the protestors, was reason enough to show concern. They rightfully believe that ill-gotten fame should not warrant political endorsements — even when that fame is used for good. Therefore, applauding Nelly for using his fame to support the school system is in essence an endorsement of the route he took to attain fame and should yield the same righteous indignation reserved for a philanthropic drug dealer. Not government honors!

Fortunately, hip-hop reform leaders like Najee Ali understand this principle. In his capacity as director of a Los Angeles-based civil-rights organization, Ali has spearheaded several well-publicized protests and boycotts to combat the indiscretions of hip-hop's major icons.

One such protest was levied against Snoop Dogg for his scheduled cameo appearance on the 2002 Muppets Christmas television special. After learning of the inappropriate plans to parade a gangster rapper who doubles as a porn icon in front of millions of impressionable adolescent viewers, Ali publicly admonished The Jim Henson Company. The company subsequently announced Snoop Dogg's removal from the television special due to sudden, suspicious time constraints.

Despite the company's claim that the tactics to foil Snoop Dogg's appearance on the Muppets special were inconsequential, Ali's every utterance in opposition of their decision to cast a foul-mouthed rapper to entertain children was absolutely necessary.

Ali and a growing number of other less-celebrated activists are justly demanding that the entertainment industry subscribe to an unwritten moral code of absolutes that are undergirded by a sense of social responsibility. More importantly, their significance is solidified by their unyielding commitment to vehemently protest and boycott icons that cross the line of decency and threaten to disrupt society's moral fabric. Therefore, the ability of these activists to shine a morally astute light at an industry that harbors such a numb conscience should not be taken lightly.

But despite all the good attempted by these hip-hop protesters, they can't escape the laws of activism, which teaches that there is always a threatening antithesis lurking in the shadows of righteousness.

James Earl Ray was the deadly nemesis who lurked in the shadow of Dr. King's civil-rights initiatives. Vietnam War proponents were thorns in the side of Muhammad Ali's declaration for peace. And an angry Jewish lynch mob was the bone of contention that sought to spoil the salvation mission of Jesus Christ.

It should come as no surprise, therefore, that hard-core left-wing proponents bent on preserving the status quo make a habit of lambasting the outspoken critics of hip-hop's decadent characteristics. These enthusiasts serve as the threatening antithesis to hip-hop's restoration movement. Unfortunately, in that role, they create a host of stereotypical classifications that unfairly attempt to pigeonhole restoration activists as watchdogs, rampant conservatives, or religious fanatics.

To further strengthen their arsenal against activists they learn to slyly shift discussions to ones of social priorities to avoid debating the merit of sound principles. "Aren't there more important social issues for them to address?" hip-hop proponents commonly ask after losing footing in debates regarding responsible entertainment.

Because of their lack of ability to stand on the legitimacy of their philosophies, they employ a diversionary tactic that calls into question the importance of other worldly injustices. They ask, "What about homelessness, AIDS, terrorist attacks, and racial profiling? Shouldn't these issues take precedence over hip-hop boycotts?"

Unfortunately, this tactic of balancing hip-hop against other social epidemics causes many would-be diehard restoration advocates to take a softer stance against the culture's indiscretions. They wouldn't, however, if they understood that addressing social ills isn't a solo sport. Instead, it takes a team of committed leaders to effectively confront the wrongs of the world.

Just like a rational basketball fan shouldn't expect a colossal-sized center like Shaquille O'Neal to play out of his position by guarding a small, nibble guard like Allen Iverson for the duration of a game, neither should people expect hip-hop restoration activists to reprioritize their agendas to permanently accommodate other social ills. This doesn't suggest that AIDS, homelessness, racism, and economic disparity aren't important issues. They are! But to neglect one important social shortcoming for another does nothing more than create voids in areas that desperately require the attention of concerned, responsible activists. To ignore any social discrepancy could be a costly mistake.

Therefore, all activists should subscribe to a holistic philosophy that allows leaders to use their different gifts to fulfill their individual missions. Those who have accepted the call to serve as spiritual leaders must make it their prerogative to help hone righteous moral constitutions among those they influence. Political leaders must unwaveringly defend the honorable laws and policies that govern our communities. And educational leaders must be blinded by the task of producing competent students to infiltrate society's blind spots.

All activists must consume themselves with the single mission of fashioning strategies to address the wrongs in the area they feel most passionate. This holistic approach creates the necessary social balance and proper context for hip-hop activism. It allows activists to address the shortcomings of hip-hop without facing feelings of guilt for placing other social ills lower on their priority list.

Hey, DJ Don't Play That Song

Ray Griffith is the concerned father of a teenage daughter. Like in many middle-class households his child gets out of school hours before his workday ends. But instead of making her a latchkey kid like millions of other children, Griffith refuses to give his daughter access to the house when he or his wife isn't home.

His decision to make the house off limits to his daughter is not the result of any sophomoric antics on her part. In fact, he's proud of how she is developing into a responsible, intelligent young lady and wants to do all he can to keep her on this progressive track.

For that reason, Griffith has made it his parenting prerogative to ban his daughter from the house in order to limit her unsupervised access to radio and music video programs that irresponsibly cater to youth audiences.

"The airwaves aren't safe anymore" for parents committed to raising their children responsibly, according to Griffith. It's now a dangerous gamble to use the television or radio as a surrogate babysitter because the programmers who select the songs and music videos for youth-oriented shows take an irresponsible approach to their jobs.

The growing number of profane songs aired on the radio and salacious music videos paraded before children in prime-time hours is a clear indication that programmers now exercise a blatant disregard for the welfare of their core hip-hop demographic.

Because concerned adults like Griffith understand that what children hear is what they'll cheer, it's important that he and others across the country make concerted efforts to challenge the gatekeepers of hip-hop airwaves to adhere to a higher level of programming standards. Radio and music video programmers should be required to adhere to the following principles:

1.   Consider the consequences

The reality of hip-hop is that every expression it makes leaves an impression on its listeners. For better or worse, programmers are in a powerful position to determine what impressions its young listeners will receive.

If these programmers considered the societal outcome if their listeners subscribed wholeheartedly to the lyrical content in the songs they grant airtime they should produce better playlists. Therefore, programmers should be challenged to administer a litmus test to songs and videos considered for airtime to determine if they contribute to the betterment or detriment of youth audiences.

2. Mentor through music

Because it does take a village to raise a child, urban radio and music video programmers should use their influential positions to mentor youths with the music they select for airplay. The growing number of single mothers and absentee fathers is a child-rearing travesty that requires a commitment from society to fill mentoring gaps for the millions of children who are deprived of worthy role models. And because statistics tell us that these children are influenced mostly by the media they consume, it should behoove programmers to pay better attention to the icons they place before them as well as to the frequency with which they do so.

This challenge of mentoring through music requires programmers to intentionally select music that uplifts and inspires youths to strive for greatness rather than mediocrity.

3. Tame the playlists

It's rare to listen to an urban radio station or watch a hip-hop music video that hasn't undergone some form of special lyrical editing. These songs are usually ripe with profanity and crude sexual references that wouldn't meet FCC standards in their original form. Therefore, choice words are edited out and forbidden content is rephrased to make many hip-hop songs friendlier.

Unfortunately, the abrasive edges on many of these songs remain even after the edits. Bleeping out a sexual reference in a rhyme preceded by the word "duck" does little to alter its impact, for instance. Young hip-hop fans are sophisticated enough to unravel such an elementary mystery. Such is the case with the majority of recent hip-hop songs that find their way onto public airwaves. They have the uncanny ability to leave little to the imagination with regards to profanity and obscenity.

The danger in this modern phenomenon is that it not only pollutes the airwaves, but it helps contaminate the unguarded minds of vulnerable listeners. To remedy the problem, programmers must accept the challenge to tame their playlists by avoiding songs that require special editing to "clean up" the lyrics.

4. Set the standard

In order to tame their playlists, programmers (along with radio and television station owners) must accept and understand their roles as the most important trendsetters within the entertainment industry.

The reality of the industry is that there will always be many more record companies with songs that vie for airtime than there will ever be radio stations to *grant* them all airtime.

That simple mathematic equation creates for programmers an unimaginable degree of power that isn't being properly stewarded. In fact, this disproportionate ratio has created an unscrupulous "pay for play" practice in the industry that is facing serious scrutiny from radio reformists. With the power to determine what songs will receive airtime amongst the hundreds of thousands produced every year, programmers have an unparalleled ability to weave a healthier social tapestry for susceptible hip-hop fans by selecting more appropriate songs for their consumption. Not even chart toppers Eminem, Jay-Z, Ja Rule, and P. Diddy have the collective ability to impact hip-hop fans like programmers do.

And because the success of these artists and record companies is largely contingent upon the willingness of media outlets to prioritize their music, programmers must take advantage of their authority to demand better music and videos.

5. Make nighttime the right time

If programmers, for some Godforsaken reason, believe they must include questionable hip-hop songs on their playlists, they should be challenged to play those songs and videos during nighttime hours when young fans are most likely to be asleep.

Programmers should be willing to grant concerned parents like Ray Griffith the courtesy of knowing that their children won't be inundated with risqué hip-hop music when they can't be there to regulate their listening and viewing consumption.

6. Promote decency

It's no surprise that parents often reward their children for good behavior. In fact, in many households, good grades are synonymous with new clothes, money, and special privileges. The rationale of this philosophy is for parents to reinforce the behavior they most desire from their children.

The motive behind this principle is one that radio station programmers should be challenged to adopt as they decide what music will fill the airwaves. Consider the radical change that might occur within hip-hop circles if radio stations rewarded local amateur artists with airtime for exhibiting a great sense of decency and creativity within their music.

That gesture alone would reinforce a healthier hip-hop community because artists would be inclined to clean up their acts to vie for airtime. In addition, it helps ensure that the next "big" hip-hop act to emerge from the amateur ranks builds a following based on its standards of decency, which ultimately could impact the genre as a whole.

7. Connect with the community

Promoting decency among local amateur artists can only occur when programmers connect with the communities they serve. Distancing themselves from the people who support their shows and those greatly impacted by the music they air is a mistake that can have dangerous repercussions.

Therefore, it would behoove radio stations to partner with local organizations to host and sponsor quarterly town hall meetings in which concerned citizens can share ideas about how stations might better serve the community. Citizens could also learn the rationale behind programming decisions at certain stations.

No greater example of reciprocal support could exist between the community and radio stations than when they understand one another's needs and make the necessary adjustments to accommodate them.

The Heart of the Matter

This book has provided numerous examples to prove that hip-hop is no longer the obscure, novelty act birthed in the streets of New York City during the late 1970s. It is now a ubiquitous culture that influences millions of fans in many countries around the world.

And as hip-hop has evolved, so have its agendas. In its infancy, the culture was driven by the intoxicating lure of two turntables and a microphone. It underwent a metamorphosis by adopting a socially conscience agenda that took pride in being black and found courage in challenging social injustices.

Hip-hop's next growth spurt ushered us into the thug

life era, when gang colors became fashion staples and blatant disregards for human life were applauded anomalously. The next stop on the hip-hop train was in party-ville, where the champagne never stopped flowing and the party's didn't stop "'til six in the morning." And the latest chapter in the life of hip-hop is the bling-bling age, where $300,000 cars come a dime a dozen and diamond-encrusted platinum jewelry is standard paraphernalia.

A haphazard concoction of these agendas (with a strong emphasis on the latter three) makes up the current state of hip-hop, which consequently is in an unsurprising state of emergency. But flashes of mature activism among hip-hop innovators suggest that the culture may be embarking upon a new era of responsibility.

Take, for instance, the slew of hip-hop summits taking place across the country that are engaging entertainers, executives, ministers, and politicians in discussions about restoring order to the culture.

Or consider the itemized political agenda of The Hip-Hop Summit Action Network, created to influence local and federal legislative agendas.

And no hip-hop connoisseur could ignore the significance of the two most prominent name changes in the industry. First, longtime gangster rapper Scarface changed his stage name to Face in a move that distanced him from the vicious movie character from which his name was derived.

Second, Suge Knight attempted to remove the stigma from his infamous record company by changing its name from Death Row Records to Tha Row Records.

These promising instances, and many others like them, give hope that a better day may be dawning for hip-hop. After all, the optimistic undertones reverberating throughout the industry do have the potential to create new results by inspiring trendsetters to produce better products and images. But it would be foolish to expect a substantive hip-hop revolution to occur without a meticulous strategy to align the most critical aspect of the movement with its most potent ventures.

The truth is—no matter how many hip-hop summits take place, no matter how honorable hip-hop political agendas become, and no matter how frequently politically correct name changes occur—hip-hop cannot be expected to reroute its course of destruction until a change occurs within the moral compasses of those who influence the culture. In other words, the heart of the hip-hop problem is the problem of the hip-hop heart.

To solve hip-hop's crisis, an exorcism must be performed on the hip-hop heart. Conversely, to address the *symptoms* of the heart problem without first addressing the shortcomings of the heart is a mistake that will lead to an ineffective hip-hop reconstruction strategy.

This alignment philosophy is built on the same premise as proper shirt buttoning. It's well understood that if the first button of a shirt isn't placed in the correct buttonhole the entire shirt will be misaligned. And everyone knows that repositioning subsequent buttons without correcting the first misaligned button is futile. Hence, it is of utmost importance to properly align the first button.

This same principle also applies to hip-hop reconstruction strategies. If the hearts of the leaders and trendsetters of hip-hop aren't bound by righteous standards they are guaranteed to produce lackluster social results. That's because their hearts are the first buttonholes in the hip-hop reconstruction alignment.

Therefore, if future hip-hop summits don't include strategies to claim the hearts of the culture's trendsetters they will ultimately be rendered ineffective no matter how well attended they are because the proverbial first button is in the wrong buttonhole.

Likewise, it would be all for naught if hip-hop political action committees were to persuade legislators to embrace their agendas and fail to properly align the hearts of their hip-hop constituencies. Again, the alignment would buckle because the first button isn't properly placed.

And the politically correct gesture of assuming less threatening names is a tactic that will bear little to no long-term benefit because it can't substitute the need for substantive change.

Any worthy cause like hip-hop reconstruction will only be as successful as the passion and sincerity of the people who fuel it. To the surprise of many, money and celebrities in such movements play second fiddle to the effectiveness of these two X factors. Audiences can sense sincerity. They can feel passion. And when they do, they're more apt to lend support to leaders who exude these contagious traits.

Therefore, the overdue hip-hop revolution will continue to lie dormant until the icons of the culture merge their strategies for external support with sincere internal desires to move in a more honorable direction. And the laws of revolution teach that these two threatening enemies within hip-hop's external and internal circles must be conquered before the holistic change that's needed within the hip-hop industry can occur.

The first enemy is the one from without. For hip-hop, these external enemies are often watchdog organizations, concerned parents, ambitious politicians, and irritated civil-rights organizations. These are the groups that typically pressure hip-hop icons to set better standards for themselves.

The second and most significant enemy that must be conquered to ensure a successful holistic hip-hop revolution is the enemy from within. These enemies are the hip-hop insiders who, through unruly behavior, stifle the potential to move the culture to higher ground. By their egregious acts, these enemies have the power to hold the culture hostage in an idle breeding ground of excuses.

Typically, the inclination of most hip-hoppers is to use the lion's share of their resources to fight the enemy from without. The danger of this strategy is that it eventually becomes self-defeating. Because when and if the enemies from without acquiesce to hip-hop demands, insiders who haven't been prepared for the revolution aren't usually in a position to make the most of their new privileges.

Take, for instance, the Civil Rights movement that challenged the racist enemies from without to extend voting privileges to African Americans. Although the movement was successful at securing voting rights, the bittersweet realization is that nearly 50 percent of the African American enemies from within didn't vote in the 2000 presidential election.

A similar, if not worse, fate awaits hip-hop if it can't convince its internal enemies to forsake the unruly habits that prevent the culture from fulfilling its greatest potential. If it doesn't, the hip-hop restoration movement will be an exercise in futility because it can't fix what it won't face.

The good news in this grim forecast is that there are hip-hop artists who have made radical changes in their public personas after assessing the internal and external damage of their lyrics and images. The rapper formerly known as Gangsta Boo is one of them. She did a surprising about-face after taking an honest, introspective look at herself. Today, she's no longer the female lyrical bandit for the toxic group Three 6 Mafia. Instead, she performs under the new moniker Lady Boo to indicate that she's sincerely "toned it down a lot."

If Lady Boo, Mason Betha, Reverend Run, and other righteous icons can serve as Pied Pipers for their colleagues who have contributed to the infestation of hip-hop, the culture could be redeemed. But let there be no mistake about it, their task of winning over hip-hop's wayward characters isn't an easy one.

The greatest obstacle in rehabilitating troubling hip-hop artists may be helping those of affluent persuasions overcome the parallel hazards of the African Monkey Trapping Technique. Instead of using painful trappings to capture wild monkeys, African hunters lure the primates with a simple but powerful psychological understanding. The hunters cut holes in coconuts and place food inside of them, knowing that monkeys will eventually stick their hands inside to get the food out. When they do, the monkeys clinch the food in their palms, which makes an enlarged fist that won't slide out of the coconut as easily as it slid in.

It's the greed of the monkeys that eventually renders them vulnerable because they won't let go of the food in the coconut long enough to free themselves. To be clear, it is the monkeys' inability to let go that hinders what would otherwise be an easy escape from the hunters, who eventually subdue them.

Likewise, in many instances it's the glittery trappings of hip-hop that prevent its rebellious insiders from fleeing the culture's dangerous pitfalls. They just won't let go. They won't let go of the money. They won't let go of the fame. They won't let go of the power.

If these artists understood, however, that incentives don't make bad deals good, they would be much more inclined to release their tight grip on the dishonorable traits of the industry.

If they understood that million-dollar contracts don't make the act of degrading women admirable, they might reconsider their "money over bitches" outbursts. If they understood that the promise of fame doesn't make the decision to glorify drugs honorable, they might get off their "high 'til I die" soap boxes. And if they understood that the potential for power doesn't make the act of pandering immoral sex any less egregious, they might mute their "freaky tales."

But far too often they *don't* understand. As a result, they naturally blend into the current hip-hop scenery along with the many other pollutants of the culture. What's needed, instead, is for more artists to rewire their hearts and stand out like the phrase I once observed in a restaurant bathroom.

Amidst a wall covered in typical bathroom obscenities was a rather peculiar confession. It wasn't the standard "For a good time, call Jane Doe." Neither was it the potty-mouthed poem "Here I sit all broken hearted." But surrounded by a mural of such obscenities, was the phrase "I like math!"

How odd! "I like math!"

What a strange confession to make in a place typically reserved for lewd, salacious declarations. It stood out like a person wearing a tuxedo at a hip-hop concert. Or better yet, it was a ray of light on an otherwise dark wall of profanity. And it was there because some arithmetic lover chose to be bold and different in an environment saturated with immorality.

Hip-hop would do well to mimic this maverick. The culture's protective walls are currently laced with restroom obscenities that unfortunately have become the norm. And the reality is that hip-hop will never recover from its degenerate state until its champions dare to be different and confess their proverbial love for math.

About the Author

DEVONE HOLT is the author and producer of the *Against All Odds Report* (www.AAOReport.com), a biweekly column created to protect and promote healthy images and messages within the entertainment industry. As a lecturer, columnist, and director of Kentucky's largest African American Christian men's ministry, his message of integrity-based entertainment is heard and read by thousands. He lives in Louisville, Kentucky, with his wife, Dionne.